# THE
# FULL FEE
# AGENT

CHRIS VOSS AND STEVE SHULL

# THE
# FULL FEE
# AGENT

*How to Stack the Odds in Your Favor*
*as a Real Estate Professional*

**The Full Fee Agent**

*How to Stack the Odds in Your Favor as a Real Estate Professional*

ISBN   978-1-5445-3663-7 *Hardcover*
       978-1-5445-4085-6 *Paperback*
       978-1-5445-3664-4 *Ebook*
       978-1-5445-3665-1 *Audiobook*

*"Real estate agents are the greatest bargain on planet earth."*

—Chris Voss

*We would like to dedicate this book to every*

*real estate professional who truly wants to excel in this business.*

*Every day, you go out into the world, working hard to be trustworthy,*

*competent, and a straight shooter, with little or no appreciation.*

*Most of your clients undervalue your service and think they can do*

*your job better than you. It is virtually impossible for any buyer*

*or seller to fully understand the complexity of your*

*efforts and the skill and knowledge required.*

*If they only walked one day in your shoes, perhaps*

*they would have a very different opinion.*

*Hopefully this book will give you the insight and wisdom to*

*conduct your business to the best of your ability, and live with*

*less stress and greater ease in everything you do.*

—Steve Shull

**IT IS NOT ABOUT GETTING IT DONE...
IT'S ABOUT DOING IT EVERY DAY.**

# CONTENTS

**FOREWORD**   *ix*
*Elaine Stucy*

**INTRODUCTION**   *1*

Chapter 1
**IGNORE HUMAN NATURE AT YOUR PERIL**   *17*

Chapter 2
**THE FAVORITE OR THE FOOL**   *33*

Chapter 3
**NO MORE FREE CONSULTING**   *59*

Chapter 4
**GET THE ELEPHANTS OUT EARLY**   *81*

Chapter 5
**PUT THE RESPONSIBILITY WHERE IT BELONGS**   *105*

Chapter 6
**LET THEM SAY NO**  *119*

Chapter 7
**NAIL THE LASTING IMPRESSION**  *133*

Chapter 8
**BE A FULL-SERVICE, FULL FEE AGENT**  *147*

**CONCLUSION**  *175*

**ACKNOWLEDGMENTS**  *187*

**ABOUT THE AUTHORS**  *191*

# FOREWORD

## Elaine Stucy

DECEMBER 12, 2000 WAS THE EVENING MY LIFE CHANGED FOREVER. Desperately in need of improvement in my sales results, I contacted Steve Shull, a business coach I had heard on a conference call. He sounded strong, confident, even intimidating. It didn't matter, I urgently needed direction. Did I say direction? Instead, I got an earthquake! Steve initiated a radical about-face in my career and life. In one remarkable—and very short—conversation, the man showed me the blue-sky potential of a career in real estate. I believed him. He changed my direction all right... and transformed my life.

After that conversation, I knew better than to expect anything conventional from Steve's coaching. That was twenty-one years ago, and to this day, he can't let it rest. Steve is still a man on a mission of discovery into how to help real estate brokers become the best of the best and enjoy the process.

In my early years, his coaching was all about discipline, focus, and goals. He relentlessly taught me how to create $1 million a year in revenue. Steve instilled belief—not blind faith, but credibility worth trusting. Whatever he told me to do, I jumped in with both feet, usually with great results. Over the years, I built a boutique brokerage and sold to a major brokerage firm, where I still practice.

When Chris came on board a few years ago, it took things to a whole new level. What we were doing had been working well, but Chris's insight into human behavior was like rocket fuel. Steve went all in, so I did too, and the resulting transformation made my business more successful and sustainable than I ever imagined.

Above all, Steve has uncanny insight and perception. He is always learning, investigating, experimenting, and improving, and he sees to the heart of situations and people in startling ways.

A recurring lament from Steve is that no matter the level of success, or lack thereof, his clients share puzzling maladies. Why such constant stress and drama in agents' lives? Why are agents always operating out of fear? How is it that many are afraid to take a day off (you know who you are), reluctant to tell clients when they are taking a vacation, making everything personal, striving constantly to be liked, cutting fees to get business, worried, attached to every outcome, determined to convince, or too superstitious or fearful to try something different? A small percentage transcend, but most suffer.

Steve always admonished us that there is no magic pill in real estate. On that prescription, he may be proving himself wrong. He and Chris are giving the real estate world a book with all the effects of a magic pill, a great elixir. Oh, it might be hard to swallow for some. It takes courage and spirit to let go of practices that don't work well, to open up and absorb a new way. It takes even more courage and faith to suspend resistance, and believe there is an even better way when what you do is working. Within these pages is the extraordinary wisdom to create a bridge of trust between people, and make the process of a real estate career a wholly beneficial, joyful experience. I hope you have the courage to try.

# INTRODUCTION

*How you do business is more important
than how much business you do.*

On a Saturday afternoon in the fall of 2016, everything I thought I knew about selling real estate went out the window.

I was by no means new to the business. Over the previous twenty-five years, I had sold real estate in high volume, grown real estate startups and training companies, and owned a successful real estate brokerage that I helped build from scratch. Most importantly, I had coached the best of the best in the industry for decades, constantly perfecting my methods to help agents take the next step in their business and reach heights they once thought impossible. I studied real estate agents nonstop, and there was probably no one else on the planet earth who understood them better.

After living and breathing real estate for that long, I was convinced I had this thing wired from beginning to end. If you wanted a straightforward blueprint for achieving greatness, I served it up on a platter...or so I thought.

I was wrong. That day, I realized I had to rewrite the playbook from scratch.

It wasn't the first time I found myself taking on a radical life change virtually overnight. I did it when a knee injury cut my professional football career short after just four years with the Miami Dolphins. I did it when I finished my MBA and took a job on Wall Street, and again when I left that job to start my own trading company with a colleague.

The world of finance wasn't my final stop, though. Sometime in 1990, someone gave me a recorded interview of two Long Beach, California real estate agents, Kim and Daryl Rouse. This duo was articulate, energetic, and dynamic. They had a plan, they knew how to execute it, and in just their second year as agents, they were on track to sell one hundred homes. Given that the average agent sells four to six homes per year, that was impressive stuff.

As I listened to the interview, something clicked inside me. Everything they were saying made total sense. It was all repeatable. I could envision myself doing the same thing, and generating the same result.

That was all the spark I needed for another radical change. So in 1991, I packed up all my belongings and headed to Southern California —Fullerton, to be exact. I didn't know anyone or anything about real estate, but the interview with Kim and Daryl just kept playing in my head: contacts equal leads...leads equal appointments...appointments equal listings...listings equal sales!

That progression was going to be my new life. I was a man on a mission, and as usual for me, there was no Plan B—I just assumed I would succeed. (Some say that successful people have a certain delusional quality about them, and I tend to agree.)

I wasn't trying to reinvent the wheel. I attended many seminars and workshops, listened intently to one top agent after another, and did exactly what they were doing. I was motivated, disciplined, and looking for any edge I could get. Because of my sports background, I was no stranger to hard work and didn't struggle with the idea that I needed to prospect three to five hours a day. My goal was to make fifty contacts every day, and that was simply what had to get done.

I could hardly have picked a worse year to start this career. At one point, my partner and I had forty listings and no escrows. If four people walked into an open house, it was a huge success. "Multiple offers" meant buyers were writing offers on multiple properties to see where they could get the best deal. Most listings took somewhere between ninety days and a year to sell—if they sold at all. Times were scary, and it was hard not to second guess my decision to become a real estate agent.

But after knocking on 200 doors a day, five days a week, and calling every expired listing every day, the momentum finally kicked in. By the end of 1991, my first year in real estate, my partner and I had closed fifty-three transactions in one of the most difficult markets ever.

In my second year, I came up with the idea of creating a coaching program for agents. I knew what worked, I had put it into practice, and I believed I could help other people do the same. To my knowledge, at that point, there was no such thing as real estate coaching—plenty of speakers and trainers, but no coaches.

So, I teamed up with one the biggest speakers in the business, and that's how the first real estate coaching program was born. It took off almost immediately. When we first introduced the program to a

Coldwell Banker office in Las Vegas, we signed up nine agents. Then, at a much larger workshop in San Francisco, we signed up ninety more.

The original format was a fifteen-minute phone call every other week for one hundred dollars per month, and agents completed a daily activity report and faxed it to me every week. The fax machine was going nonstop, as were my coaching calls. Soon, my schedule was filled with clients, and we hired nine other full-time coaches.

*This* was what I was meant to do—not sell real estate myself but help other agents become the best they could be. I'm a coach at heart, and my curiosity and desire to figure out this industry never fades. So, in 1996, I went out on my own and formed Performance Coaching, and I stayed the course for two decades...until that day in the fall of 2016.

That was the day I started reading a book a coaching client had given to me: *Never Split the Difference* by Chris Voss (the coauthor of this book). In that bestseller, Chris shared the negotiation strategies he had learned over two decades as a hostage negotiator for the FBI. When the book came out in 2016, it completely upended the prevailing wisdom on negotiation, calling into question the logic-driven, yes-focused methods everyone took for granted. Since then, it has become the go-to guide for business negotiators everywhere, and Chris is one of the most sought-after negotiation trainers in the world.

The title was what drew me in. Never split the difference? In real estate deals, agents almost *always* ended up splitting the difference! If that was a flawed strategy, I had to find out why. Just like the 1990 interview with the two Long Beach agents, Chris's book turned out to be a life changer.

Up to that point, I had viewed real estate as a linear process, just as

I had been taught from the beginning. Nuts and bolts 101. Looking at the business through the lens of fact, logic, and reason, everything could be synthesized into a foolproof series of clearly defined actions. There was no emotional component to my calculations because emotions just got in the way of rationality.

Big mistake.

Thanks to Chris, I finally saw what I had been overlooking: **you can't overcome emotion with fact, logic, and reason.**

Chris's message hit me like a lightning bolt. The approach I had been using for my entire career was completely backwards. I had been trying to eliminate the volatile emotions inherent in the real estate business, but that's impossible—it's simply against human nature. *You can't overcome emotion with fact, logic, and reason.*

## FOMO AND THE TEMPTATION OF MORE

In short, I had gotten really good at doing the wrong thing. It worked— my clients got great results...but only by repeatedly conquering a problem they could have been avoiding altogether.

I call that problem the agent's doom loop: chase, convince, and close.

Virtually every agent lives in this cycle. It's not what you signed up for—if you're like most agents, you got into this industry to earn a six-figure income, be your own boss, and have flexibility in your schedule. But in reality, that six-figure income is elusive, being your own boss is harder than you ever imagined, and "flexibility" really means being on call 24/7.

Why? Because of fear.

That's the real driving force in the residential real estate industry. To be more precise, it's the fear of missing out (a.k.a. FOMO). Why else do you work the way you work? You don't chase on a daily basis for the thrill of it. You don't convince because you love twisting arms. You don't take every opportunity to close because you think people love being pressured.

You do all this because you fear what will happen if you don't. As human beings, we've been conditioned to believe that our inside world is directly related to the outside world. As a result, we spend our entire lives trying to get the outside world to line up in a way that makes us feel good on the inside. If we can achieve certain external results, we'll finally be happy.

That's a nice story, but it's simply not true. In reality, the inside and outside world operate independently from each other. The world will go on the way it does regardless of how you feel about it, and no external results will ever bring the lasting joy and inner peace you crave in your life.

This isn't just idle philosophy—the doom loop is a direct byproduct of this false way of thinking. You're a commissioned salesperson. You only get paid when you close a sale. The prospect of not getting that result sends your mind to all the dark places. Unconsciously, you think that your business will fail...you'll go broke...you'll starve...you'll *die*. This may sound like a gross exaggeration, but for most real estate agents, this is their life. No money equals death.

This way of thinking and feeling puts you in full-on survival mode. You chase, convince, and close as if your life depends on it because in your mind, it actually does. But the more you follow this doom loop, the more you push people away, which then fuels more feelings around lack and limitation. It's a never-ending cycle of doom and gloom.

So, with a market that's overflowing with licensed agents, fear has you running ragged in search of legitimate opportunities, trying to grab a piece of the pie before it disappears.

The problem is, most of your leads turn out to be wild goose chases that never turn into real business. In fact, probably 80 percent of your time gets wasted on work that generates exactly zero revenue (but plenty of frustration and heartbreak).That high-cost, low-return activity is a drain on your time, energy, and bank account, but it feels like a require-ment. How else are you supposed to get any clients?

So you chase, chase, chase. Convince, convince, convince. Close, close, close. Rinse and repeat.

And the solution to every problem always feels the same: just do one more deal. How many times have you said it to yourself? *If I can just do one more deal, everything will be okay.* Forget "location, location, location"—the true refrain in this business is "more, more, more!"

Would it be ridiculous to say all the training you've received has been focused on how to get some version of "more" in your business? More contacts, leads, appointments, buyers, listings, sales, money, mar-ket share, rankings, time, people working for you. Fill in the blank as you like.

It's hard to not be seduced by the prospect of more. It sounds so wonderful...but it's usually a trap. More rarely solves anything. It only leads to more desire. If you do what you've been taught, you might increase your productivity, but the stress and struggle will not disappear. Ultimately, you'll be left in the same place you are now, wanting and thinking you need to do more. It's a never-ending cycle that leads to mental and emotional exhaustion.

On top of that, whether you realize it or not, every force imaginable is conspiring to turn you into a commodity. This is the biggest trap of all, and no one is immune. Industry "best practices" manipulate you into thinking that to win business, you must work harder, spend more money, give away your most valuable information, promise more than you can deliver, and charge less than you deserve. You're forced into a transactional perspective that pits your ambition against your integrity.

That's a formula for burnout if there ever was one.

## THE MISSING PIECE

You know who doesn't burn out?

Tom Brady.

Even if you've never watched a single football game in your life, I bet you know who he is: the winningest quarterback in NFL history, with more Super Bowl victories (seven) than any other player *or* team. In twenty-two seasons in the NFL, he has suffered only one serious injury, and at age forty-four, he shows no signs of slowing down.

That longevity is no accident, and it has more to do with *your* longevity in real estate than you might think.

As Brady explained in his book, *The TB12 Method: How to Achieve a*

*Lifetime of Sustained Peak*, the normal cycle for athletes is to train, play, get hurt, and rehab, over and over. The problem is that typical fitness models emphasize strength and conditioning but are missing another crucial piece: pliability. Pliability removes the tension and stress from the training process, eliminating the main cause of injury.

- In *Never Split the Difference*, I found the missing piece for real estate agents: *Tactical Empathy*.

To explain what that means, let me back up a step. Remember, you can't overcome emotion with fact, logic, and reason...but you can work *with* those emotions to do business in a more authentic and effective way. You can learn from what works in other high-stakes, emotional situations (like the hostage negotiations Chris knows so well), and use it to make the real estate business work better for everyone—you *and* the buyers and sellers who hire you.

I can't emphasize it enough: emotion is what really drives decisions in real estate. You're shepherding buyers and sellers through one of the most stressful and significant decisions of their lives, and everyone's hopes and dreams are on the line. Buyers are hoping to find the perfect home for a bargain, and sellers are hoping to make a boatload of money on the asset they've been lovingly maintaining for years. On top of that, you want a painless deal that satisfies everyone, pays you a respectable commission, and generates repeat and referral business in the future.

But when it comes to sales training for agents, the science and skill of dealing with emotions (both yours and those of your prospects and clients) is practically nonexistent. Scripted presentations, objection handlers, and closing dialogues still rule the day. Emotional intelligence rarely gets a mention, and empathy never.

Instead, you're taught to win clients by explaining your value: your track record, market insight, pricing strategy, resources, connections, time commitment, and of course, your discounted fee. One by one, you present the factual, logical reasons why you're the best for the job...and your prospects smile and thank you profusely and never call you again. Every conversation is like an unwinnable tug-of-war: you're trying to pull them over to your side with fact, logic, and reason, but the harder you pull, the more they resist.

How many times have you left an appointment with no clue whether you had a real shot at getting the listing? How many times did you think you had it in the bag, only to find out later that they went with someone else? Why does this happen?

Because you didn't make them feel understood.

Not that you didn't understand them. I'm sure you did. You just didn't make them *feel understood.*

It's almost the same thing Stephen Covey said in *The 7 Habits of Highly Effective People*: "Seek first to understand, then to be understood." What he forgot to mention was that understanding doesn't count for anything until the *other person believes* you understand them. You know what they say when that happens?

**"That's right."**

As in, "That's right, you are now seeing the world from my perspective and speaking my language. You get me."

Reaching "that's right" requires **Tactical Empathy**: the art of influencing others by articulating what they're thinking and feeling, without necessarily agreeing, disagreeing, or sympathizing.

---

### Tactical Empathy

The art of influencing others by articulating what they're thinking and feeling, without necessarily agreeing, disagreeing, or sympathizing.

---

Just as pliability removes tension from athletic training, Tactical Empathy takes the stress out of real estate sales. It cuts off the agent's doom loop before it even starts—no more endless rounds of chasing, convincing, and closing.

## FROM EXPLAINING VALUE TO BUILDING TRUST

This is what no one else is teaching. It's the master key to constructing a real estate business based on building trust instead of explaining value.

When you explain your value, you become a commodity engaged in pushing transactions. Brutal, but honest.

When you cultivate trust, you become an irreplaceable advisor who creates strong relationships that yield a constant flow of repeat and referral business. Would you be opposed to hustling less while enjoying your work more and reaping bigger financial rewards? That's what trust does for you.

Forget just surviving—the methodology you're about to learn is going to make you feel alive in a brand new way. It will teach you how to become the trusted advisor your clients want, need, and will actually hire. Our approach builds on the most comprehensive scientific understanding of how people actually make decisions.

Spoiler alert: rational calculations are just the tip of the iceberg.

Below the surface are complex layers of biases, tendencies, and other brain phenomena that often make human behavior seem anything but logical. Whether you're aware of it or not (and most people aren't), these things affect your every move, from how you interpret a client's comment to what you choose to eat for lunch. Over the last few decades, researchers have tested and explained these patterns in ways that completely change how we think about influencing people.

Foreign as these ideas may be in real estate, they've already revolutionized other industries and been validated over and over by scientific studies. What you're about to learn is a more human, authentic, and honest way to sell real estate, which is precisely why it works so well.

Just imagine: what if your ambition didn't have to compete with your integrity? What if you could work in a way that aligned with your core values, beliefs, and principles? What if you could do well, be well, and help others at the same time?

Right now, you probably feel like most of what you say to your clients and prospects falls on deaf ears. When you master Tactical Empathy—the art of making people feel understood—they will finally start to hear you. Then, instead of pushing them to follow your advice, you can gently guide them in the right direction they need to go to get what they want...with them thinking it's their idea.

This book is about one simple, inescapable truth: **how you do business is more important than how much business you do.**

It sounds crazy on the surface, but you're about to see that if you focus on the *how*, the *how much* will take care of itself.

## NEW NEURAL PATHWAYS

When Chris and I started coaching together in late 2017, I made an immediate 180-degree pivot in my coaching practice, incorporating Chris's knowledge into everything I taught my clients. I couldn't *not* do that—the truth is the truth. When you hear it, it is virtually impossible to resist.

It was a seismic shift. We were laying waste to the foundation of the real estate business, turning every norm upside down, and we didn't have any hard proof yet that it would work for this industry. It had to be the right direction, though. Human nature doesn't care what industry you're in.

Just enough people believed in our conviction that we could start proving the theory. It wasn't easy—a paradigm shift never is. At first, people tried to apply these new ideas to the old way of doing things, using new language to keep chasing, convincing, and closing better. That's not how this works. If you try to do it halfway, it will fail.

But when you do it right, it's rocket fuel for your business.

Our clients have shown us time and time again that this stuff transforms careers. They do more business, but more importantly, they do it in a better way. They have less stress and more time and energy. Every deal comes easier, and leaves all parties feeling happier when it's done. The tough conversations that used to keep them up at night now come effortlessly. Nobody wants to be a pushy salesperson, and what we teach allows them to leave that behind forever...and be *more* successful than they were before.

Agents come to us with all the usual struggles: how to win more clients, manage their workloads, navigate tough conversations, close deals faster, and get better outcomes from those deals. When they learn to use Tactical Empathy as the foundation for everything they do, all those problems start to solve themselves.

You'll see it in the real-life stories we've included in this book, and you'll find out firsthand when you try these strategies yourself. The beauty is that they work immediately. Unlike learning a new sport or musical instrument, you don't have to practice for months before you can be effective. As soon as you start using Tactical Empathy, people will start responding to you differently. It can literally change the course of your career overnight.

That said, this is a new skill, and you *will* feel awkward at first. It's not complicated, and it doesn't take any special genius, but learning to use it is going to be uncomfortable and unnatural. It will go against everything you think you know about how to do your job, and you're going to think there's no way this stuff will work...but it does.

Feel the fear, and commit to doing it anyway. Every time you do, you'll strengthen the new neural pathways in your brain, and if you keep at it, soon what was once very unnatural will become second nature. That's when radical change becomes not just possible, but inevitable.

This book touches on every aspect of your relationship with a client, from the first conversation to the last impression. In each chapter, we'll examine the usual way of doing things and see how Tactical Empathy turns it on its head—and leads to wildly better results. You'll get the combined benefit of my industry experience and Chris's unparalleled negotiation expertise, plus evidence from scientific studies and examples from the agents we coach.

Practice as you go, and by the end of the book, you'll never want to do business without Tactical Empathy again.

Chapter 1

# IGNORE HUMAN NATURE AT YOUR PERIL

*Starting now, you're on a mission*
*of fearless discovery.*

WHERE DO YOU GO WHEN YOU'RE HIGHLY EDUCATED, EXTREMELY accomplished, and interested in making a lot of money?

Sell residential real estate? Isn't that why you bought this book? Please indulge me on a short journey...

The younger me's thought? Wall Street or Silicon Valley, the American meccas of ambition and brainpower.

Why? Those are the homes of the most important investment banks and venture capital firms, which deliberately recruit the smartest of the smarty-pants from the world's top universities. They need people who can do the sophisticated analyses required to make good investment decisions, and they pay top dollar for them. You would think that with all that talent at their disposal, fact, logic, and reason would rule the day in the investment world.

Fat chance. Just look at all the companies that have skyrocketed to massive valuations, only to collapse into nothing when the hype wears out.

Take Theranos, the company that promised to revolutionize blood testing and drug delivery. It took in over $700 million in capital and reached a valuation of $9 billion on promises alone, with no hard evidence that its core technology even worked. The investors who backed Theranos and the huge healthcare companies who partnered with it heard what they wanted to hear, and chose to believe it without fully verifying the facts.

Theranos wasn't an isolated incident, although it's certainly one of the most extreme. Emotion-driven booms and busts happened with WeWork, GameStop, SunEdison, Enron...the list is long. Investors heard and saw things that sounded so wonderful, they neglected to check their sources and crunch the numbers properly.

Here's both the good news...and the bad news. Human beings are not purely rational creatures. Yes, we're capable of logic, but our emotions and instincts are powerful enough to derail that analytical thinking, often without us even noticing. Over the past few decades, advances in neuroscience have allowed scientists to show just how active the emotional brain is during the decision process. The data on human behavior in real-life decision-making situations backs this up.

Fact, logic, and reason are just one part of how people do business, and the higher the pressure, the smaller that part often is. Make no mistake—real estate is high stakes. Buying or selling a house might be the biggest financial transaction a person ever makes, and it affects every aspect of their daily lives.

Your influence won't stick until you make them feel understood. That concept is as sure as gravity. Chris and I (and the Black Swan Group), would call it a Law of Negotiation Gravity.

The first step toward your goal of having your influence stick is to learn what's really going on inside their heads. Not the pro/con, profit/loss calculations but the emotions that so often override logical reasoning. When you understand and accept these realities of the human condition, your job (and your life) will get a lot easier.

Another of the Black Swan Group's Laws of Negotiation Gravity: "Ignore human nature at your peril."

Chris and I believe so strongly in this, that in this book and for your challenges, we are going to give you the Seven Essential Truths of Human Behavior.

## SEVEN ESSENTIAL TRUTHS OF HUMAN BEHAVIOR[1]

There are whole libraries of books on human behavior, if you want to see the evidence in nitty-gritty detail. That's pretty time consuming, and you're busy, so here's a quick hit list of what you need to know, spelled out in plain English. Some of these statements may seem surprising or

---

[1] Some of these are similar to the Laws of Negotiation Gravity used by Chris Voss's Black Swan Group, and as part of the Black Swan Method. Our thinking is closely aligned with theirs, for obvious reasons. For more information, check out the Black Swan Group website at www.blackswanltd.com.

counterintuitive at first, but when you start applying them to what you see every day, you'll realize how much they explain about why people do what they do.

## 1. The best predictor of future behavior is past behavior.

This clichéd phrase bothers some people because they think it implies that people can't change, which isn't true. It doesn't—it just implies that it's *hard* for people to change, which is absolutely true. We're creatures of habit because doing things on autopilot makes it easier to function in a world with way more information and choices than even our advanced brains can handle.

There's an important nuance here—the word "behavior." We are not applying this truth to "words", specifically "words" compared to "behavior." There is an old saying, "Your actions shout so loudly in my ears I can't hear what you are saying."

This is one of the reasons why the "Yes Momentum" has been shown to be faulty.[2]

When was the last time you thought about the way you walk, talk, or think? How often do you buy the same things without even considering other options? How much of your day is taken up by routines of hygiene, exercise, food, work, and travel? It's not a bad thing. We *need*

---

[2] "A surprisingly large percentage (at least half) of our participants showed no strong inherent preference for consistency." Robert B. Cialdini, Melanie R. Trost, and Jason T. Newsom, "Preference for Consistency: The Development of a Valid Measure and the Discovery of Surprising Behavioral Implications," *Journal of Personality and Social Psychology* 69, no. 2 (1995): 318–328, https://doi.org/10.1037/0022-3514.69.2.318.

to minimize the cognitive demands of everyday activities so we can free up brainpower for the tough stuff.

What this does mean that in most situations, people (including you) are most likely to *do* what they've *done* in the past under similar circumstances. This is especially true under pressure—when stress hijacks most of our gray matter, we default back to our habits. Yet even in low-stress situations, people tend to stick with what they know because it feels comfortable and safe.

Just recognizing this helps you predict how people will behave. If you can find out what they did the last time they sold their house or made some other major decision, you'll have a big clue about what they're likely to do this time around.

Don't forget that this maxim applies to you too. This book is going to push you to break and rebuild your habits around selling real estate, and it's going to be uncomfortable. But the more you practice new behaviors, the more they *become* the past behaviors that you default to. The first time is the hardest—it only gets easier after that.

## 2. There is no such thing as a fully open mind.

In studies of B2B buyer decision-making, researchers have found that when a buyer contacts a vendor, their mind is already made up about half the time.[3] If it's not, they're more than halfway through the decision process.

---

[3] TrustRadius, *The 2021 B2B Buying Disconnect*, November 2020, https://www.trustradius .com/vendor-blog/b2b-buying-disconnect-2021?utm_source=website&utm_medium =button&utm_campaign=B2BDD2021.

The numbers are a bit shocking, but when you put yourself in the buyer's shoes, it makes perfect sense. When you make a big purchase, you don't just go straight for the salesperson. You gather information first. By the time you talk to a salesperson, you've learned enough about your options to have a pretty good idea of what you want. Your mind is no longer fully open.

Fair-minded people have a hard time embracing this. You don't want to think of yourself or others as close-minded. When you're the buyer, you tell yourself that every option is still in the running until you've made your final decision, even when you know deep down that you have a clear preference. You talk to other salespeople, thinking maybe they'll say something to sway you, but in reality, the chances of that are minuscule.

When Chris needed to hire an HR consultancy to work with his company, his accountant suggested a firm to him. He interviewed that firm and liked them, but he still talked to others to see how they might be different. He knows quite well there's no such thing as an open mind, but even he was kidding himself that he might choose someone other than his accountant's referral. Then, in the middle of a sales conversation with another candidate, he asked himself what the chances were that he would actually give that person his business. Zilch: he was always going to go with the recommendation of a trusted ally.

In the next chapter, you'll see how this changes *everything* about how you do business. It sounds like a negative thing at first—no one wants to believe they're not really in the running. In reality, though, it's the key to your freedom. If you can learn to tell when a buyer is truly considering you and when they're not, you can stop wasting your time on false opportunities.

## 3. Humans are hardwired to be negative.

It's right there in our brain structure. In our layman's assessment of studies we have seen of fMRI activity of the human brain in response to negative emotions, 70 percent of the amygdala (the part of your brain that assigns emotional importance to sensory information) is dedicated to negative emotions.[4]

This is pure evolutionary biology. Responding appropriately to danger with negative emotions like fear or anger is a lot more crucial to survival than responding to positive stimuli. So, it makes sense that our brains err on the side of caution—that's how you stay alive. Most of us don't face life-and-death threats every day anymore, but evolution hasn't caught up with modern civilization.

Most real estate agents are bogged down in negativity. They walk around waiting for the other shoe to drop, thinking about what bad thing is going to happen next: what tough conversation they'll have to have, what mistake they've made, what will upset the client.

We can't change our biology, but we can use simple tools to help mitigate that natural negativity. In those same fMRI studies, something fascinating happened. When the researchers asked the subjects to label their negative emotions, those emotions dissipated. They defused negativity

---

[4] Alex Korb, *The Upward Spiral: Using Neuroscience to Reverse the Course of Depression, One Small Change at a Time* (Oakland: New Harbinger Publications, 2015).

just by labeling it. In later chapters, you'll learn how to use this technique to make tough conversations with your clients a whole lot easier.

### 4. Fear of loss is the primary motivator of human beings.

Daniel Kahneman's Prospect Theory, which won the 2002 Nobel Prize in Economics, says that the pain of a loss is twice as powerful as the pleasure of an equivalent gain.[5] In other words, to make up for the pain of losing ten dollars, you would have to gain twenty. Financially, that puts you ten dollars ahead, but emotionally, you're even.

That means the fear of loss is a much more potent motivator than the prospect of gain. So, why is every real estate agent pitching the prospect of gain? It's a "best practice" that many people are reluctant to part with. Talking about future gain feels positive and safe; talking about potential loss feels negative and manipulative.

But in fact, the surest way to get someone to act is to make them perceive inaction as a loss. Self-help giant Tony Robbins understands this—that's why he guides people to imagine their ideal future in vivid detail, to the point where they feel like it's truly theirs. Then, if they don't take the steps required to make it real, they're *losing* that ideal future. Through visualization alone, the prospect of gain turns into the prospect of loss, and suddenly the need for action seems much stronger.

This is a crucial human foible to keep in mind when influencing clients and prospects. What seems like a complete unwillingness to

---

[5] "Loss Aversion," BehavioralEconomics.com, accessed April 8, 2022, https://www.behavioral economics.com/resources/mini-encyclopedia-of-be/loss-aversion/.

follow your advice can change in an instant when you bring a compelling prospect of loss into view.

### 5. Compromise is never equal—it's a downward spiral.

Everyone thinks compromise is the way to make a fair deal. You give a little, I give a little, and we come to a fair middle ground that everyone can accept, right? Even Shark Tank investor Kevin O'Leary says a good deal is one where both sides are slightly unhappy, meaning both have compromised a little.

Well, what if I can't choose between black shoes and brown shoes? Should I compromise by wearing one of each? Of course not. That's the worst possible outcome, and the same is true for real estate deals (or any negotiation).

This goes back to Prospect Theory again. Every time you give ten dollars, you won't feel satisfied until you hit the other side for twenty, and they won't feel satisfied until they hit you for forty, and on and on. It's easy to see why both sides end up unhappy with a compromise.

Whether the deal looks good on paper or not is irrelevant. What matters is that your clients *feel bad* about it, and clients who feel bad don't recommend you to others. Compromise is killing your referral rate...which kills your pipeline and your future.

### 6. People will die over their autonomy.

"Give me liberty or give me death." It's not just a slogan of the American Revolution—it's the expression of a simple human truth. No society has ever been content in slavery.

S.W.A.T. teams learned this the hard way in their early days, when their hostage negotiation strategy was to shout, "Come out or we'll kill you!" People are kings of their castles, and given that kind of ultimatum, they often value their autonomy over their lives. So, S.W.A.T. teams all over the country ended up shooting people who didn't need to be shot.

Even when it's not a life-or-death ultimatum, no one likes to be forced into a choice. That's why persuading in the typical sense feels so uncomfortable. You feel pushy and they feel pushed, even if what you're convincing them to do is truly in their best interest. That's no way to build trust or rapport.

In later chapters, you'll learn exactly how to influence people while allowing them to stay in the driver's seat and own their choices. It doesn't just make them happier—it will make you happier too because you won't have to feel like a sleazy salesman, or take responsibility for choices that aren't yours to make.

### 7. Vision drives decision.

Consciously or otherwise, everyone has visions in their mind of what they fear and want. In virtually every situation, we imagine how things will turn out before they actually happen, anchoring our expectations based on those personal (and often unspoken) desires and worries. That vision of the future determines how we act in the present.

Let's say you've just been introduced to a new skill, something that's way outside your comfort zone. It seems difficult, and you immediately imagine yourself failing at it. You haven't even tried it yet, but your mind is already fixated on the possibility of frustration, humiliation, and disappointment. So, you decide to pass altogether.

How about a scenario we're all familiar with: a seller who has a vision that their house will sell at their inflated target price. Even if you tell them the price is too high, they're anchored on that expectation and won't budge.

Before you can influence someone, you have to know what their vision is. Most agents focus on conveying and defending their own point of view, not realizing that their vision isn't the one that matters. Your clients and prospects already have their own visions of what's going to happen, and they don't care what yours is. Your job is to see their vision, and gently nudge them to adjust it when it's out of touch with reality.

## TACTICAL EMPATHY®:
## YOUR SWISS ARMY KNIFE

Real estate brings those seven essential truths out in everyone because it's not just a transaction—it's the American dream. Owning property is part of that glorious ideal of freedom and equality, which makes it extremely emotional. Even for seasoned home owners who have bought and sold before, the deal determines not just their next home but how the next phase of their lives will look. That's heady stuff.

Every seller is hoping for more money, and every buyer is hoping for a bargain. To get as close as possible to those dreams, they're going to need you, but they won't accept your help until they know you get what they want. They want to feel seen, heard, and understood.

Thankfully, you don't need a different tactic for each one of those seven truths. They all share one solution: Tactical Empathy. Think of Tactical Empathy as the Swiss Army knife for making people feel understood. It isn't just one tool—it's a collection of tools that work together to achieve one life-changing outcome.

To see what that outcome looks like, imagine you and a client are standing on opposite sides of the street. What most agents do is shout across the street for the other person to come over...which hardly ever works. And when they try to practice understanding or empathy, it just means using their knowledge of the client to hone their argument. They're looking for the right things to say to convince the other person to cross.

That's not Tactical Empathy. In this book, what you're learning to do is cross the street, look at what they're seeing, point out some things they might have missed, and then help them navigate to where they want to go.

Night and day, right?

Not only is it vastly more effective to do business this way, but it also feels good, thanks to the brain chemistry of trust. When people feel understood, they get a hit of oxytocin, the same hormone that bonds parents and children, romantic partners, and friends. Tactical Empathy helps you form a very real bond that will endure even through the inevitable frustrations and anxieties of getting to a deal.

## THE EXPLORER MINDSET

Starting now, you're on a mission of *fearless discovery*.

There is nothing to be afraid of. None of what you're going to do is about making stuff happen—it's about embracing what's happening. You don't have to become a different person or put on a mask to be successful with this. All you have to do is set aside your desires, get curious about other people, and open yourself to being smarter today than you were yesterday.

We call this an experiment in surrendering[6]: an ongoing exercise in letting go of control and detaching yourself from the outcome of each conversation and deal.

Remember, you're not making any irrevocable decisions by trying new things. Inevitably, there will be something in this book that will violate a principle you hold dear. It's going to horrify you, and your amygdala will whisper in your ear about how it will go bad...but your amygdala is not your friend. Promise yourself now that no matter how scary it seems, you will at least try it.

You're not burning any bridges. You can always go back to your old methods if it turns out as horribly as you imagined. In our experience though, it never does.

So, don't defeat yourself before you begin. We've seen agents sit in their cars for an hour before knocking on the door, ruminating on everything that could go wrong. Why torture yourself like that? Just dive in and see what happens. It's an experiment, and you're a scientist, just observing the outcome and collecting data. No value judgment.

---

[6] Inspired in large part by Michael Singer and his book, *The Surrender Experiment*.

In those moments when it feels hard to just do it, it's helpful to think about cows and buffalo in a storm. When cows feel a storm coming, they instinctively run from it. But the storm always catches up, and they end up running right along with it, prolonging the pain and frustration. That's exactly what you're doing to yourself when you procrastinate, hesitate, and avoid the inevitable.

Buffalo, on the other hand, run straight towards the storm. By facing it head-on instead of trying to avoid it, they minimize the time they spend in the wind and rain. The hard part is over faster because they charged right into it.

So, as you practice the techniques in this book, remember that trying to avoid the tough stuff only prolongs the pain. Be the buffalo. Run into the storm.

Of course, we can't guarantee Tactical Empathy will work 100 percent of the time. Nothing does. However, Tactical Empathy will give you the best chance for success in any situation.

In Chris's experience using Tactical Empathy in hostage negotiations, his teams had a 93 percent success rate. That meant 7 percent of hostage takers were going to get shot. So, they learned to look right away for signs that the other party wasn't responding as expected.

You might find people like that, who have put up such a strong shield against empathy that they're unreceptive to this method. When you do, walk away—you don't want to work with those people. They're rare, though. Most people crave empathy, and when you learn to practice it with authenticity and confidence, you'll find that virtually everyone around you will light up in response—prospects, clients, colleagues, and even your friends and family.

That's when you'll realize this is more than a way of doing business. It's a way of living. It's a reawakening of who you really are as a human being.

It just happens to also help you build a stronger business. And now that you've seen the essential truths of how people behave, you can put that knowledge to work, starting with the very first conversation you have with a prospect.

# KEY TAKEAWAYS

→ Fact, logic, and reason are only a small part of how people make decisions. Emotions and unconscious biases play a huge role, and often make human behavior seem irrational.

→ You'll have an easier time understanding and predicting people if you remember these Seven Essential Truths of Human Behavior:

  ▷ The best predictor of future behavior is past behavior.

  ▷ There is no such thing as a fully open mind.

  ▷ Humans are hardwired to be negative.

  ▷ Fear of loss is the primary motivator of human beings.

  ▷ Compromise is never equal—it's a downward spiral.

  ▷ People will die over their autonomy.

  ▷ Vision drives decision.

→ Tactical Empathy is your Swiss Army knife for navigating human relationships and behavior.

→ As you learn to practice it throughout this book, approach the process with an attitude of fearless discovery. There's nothing to be afraid of here, and the discomfort of trying new things will disappear faster if you dive in head first.

Chapter 2

# THE FAVORITE OR THE FOOL

*It's not a sin to lose business—it's a sin to
take a long time to lose business.*

ONCE UPON A TIME IN A MAGICAL, MYSTICAL REAL ESTATE MARKET,
there lived an incredible real estate agent.

She was truly on top of her game.

She cultivated the right mindset, built strong relationships, and out-
worked everyone. Everything in her business was buttoned up tight and
state of the art. She was the personification of best practices for a real
estate professional.

One day, she received a phone call from a potential seller who asked her
to come out and give a listing presentation. It was the perfect opportunity
for the agent—this property and client fit her ideal profile for doing business.

The agent prepared everything diligently, as always. She dropped off a
pre-listing package, confirmed the appointment in advance, and arrived on
time, ready to go with a big smile and positive attitude. It was show time!

The meeting could not have gone more perfectly. The prospective sellers listened to everything she said, seemed very engaged, and asked very specific questions. Their attention never faded during the two-hour presentation.

The sellers thanked the agent profusely and commented on how impressed they were with everything she had shared. They said with a big smile, "You've given us so much to think about. Let us process everything, and we'll get back to you shortly."

The agent left the meeting on cloud nine. She desperately wanted this listing, and knew she was the best person for the job. Given that the appointment had gone even better than expected, it seemed like a sure thing. She started going through her database mentally, thinking of who she might show the property to. This was going to be fun, not to mention a great paycheck.

The next day, the phone rang. It was the seller on the line, and the agent's heart started beating rapidly in anticipation of good news...that never came.

The sellers shared again how grateful they were for all the information the agent had presented, but they had decided to work with someone else. The agent was in shock, and could barely say thank you for the call. She hung up the phone in absolute disbelief.

This made no sense. She had done everything right from start to finish. She was the obvious choice. What could have possibly happened? Did she say something wrong? Did she totally misread the situation?

**This is the story of the Favorite and the Fool.**

This version involves made-up people in a nonexistent place, but you already know it's a true story because it has happened to you (probably more times than you can count). And if you're like most agents, you're still wondering what you did wrong.

Just one thing: you assumed you actually had a shot in the first place.

You probably think I'm crazy for saying that. Of course you had a shot! Why else would they have called you and asked for a listing presentation?

What you're about to learn is that not all opportunities are created equal. Sometimes you have a high probability of doing business with a prospective client—you're the Favorite. Other times (far too often), you're the Fool. Someone else is already the Favorite, and you're just there for due diligence...wasting your time on work that will never lead to a deal, no matter what you say or do.

**The key to building a great business is learning to tell the difference between possibility and probability.** Fools chase possibilities. To be the Favorite, you have to focus on probabilities.

The concept of the Favorite and the Fool is the main organizing principle in this book. Everything else flows from this fundamental distinction. How you approach your real estate business (and the results you get from it) will change dramatically once you embrace this reality.

This is a tough pill for most agents to swallow. You're probably pushing back on this idea right now. Everyone wants to believe that if they say and do the right things, every seller will hire them, but it's simply not true.

Still skeptical? Keep reading. In this chapter, you'll see how one faulty assumption—that the playing field is level—wreaks havoc on your business every single day. More importantly, you'll learn how focusing on high-probability opportunities can transform your life, and how to start doing that *today*.

## THE OLD WAY: CHASE, CONVINCE, CLOSE

Ask yourself if any of this sounds familiar:

You get excited about every phone call from a new prospect.

On those calls, your primary objective is to get a listing appointment.

You think that the more listing appointments you go on, the more listings you'll get.

You believe prospects are making decisions based on the quality of your listing presentations, so you put a lot of time, effort, energy, and resources into them.

You know not every appointment will result in a listing, but you consider that a cost of doing business.

You chase every opportunity that crosses your path because if you don't, you might not get anything at all.

The vast majority of real estate agents think this way, so I don't blame you for doing the same. Unfortunately, it's all wrong.

Chris and I coach agents who now go on *zero* listing appointments and do more business than ever. It's not because they're superstars who are so in demand that they can afford not to do the work that "regular" people have to do. It's because they've accepted and adapted to a reality of the human condition: there's no such thing as a fully open mind[7].

The truth is, most people who contact you have no intention of ever hiring you.

They're not being deceptive or manipulative on purpose. They *think* their minds are open. But as soon as they start gathering information to make a decision, they begin to lean towards certain choices, and away from others. They start to pick a Favorite, maybe even unconsciously. Most top agents believe they are going to walk away from every listing appointment with a signed listing. Most newer agents are just happy to get a phone call. The idea that the seller has already made a decision (or is close to it) never crosses their mind.

When you're the Favorite, chances are very high (probably 80 percent or better) that you'll get the listing. It's not because of your killer presentation, though. The prospect picked you before you ever walked into that house, whether they realized it or not.

When you're not the Favorite, you're the Fool—and there is always a fool in the game. The prospect is interviewing multiple agents because it's the responsible thing to do, but it's just due diligence. They might even use the ideas and information you provide, but the chances of swaying them away from their Favorite are low (maybe 20 percent at best), even if you say and do all the right things.

---

[7] One of the Seven Essential Truths of Human Behavior.

Twenty percent isn't zero, though, and there's the danger. Sometimes, you'll win one of these low-probability listings, and that makes you believe that you can *convince* people to choose you. You start to think that if you can just make your presentation a little better—more polished, more exciting, more insightful, more packed with reasons why you're the best—you'll persuade more people to hire you. But convincing is hard work, and it doesn't feel good for you or them.

Would you rather go on a date with someone who is thrilled to be with you, or someone you had to beg? Which situation would make you feel more confident and relaxed? Which would be more enjoyable and more likely to end well?

Now, put yourself in their shoes. Would you rather go on a date with your crush, or someone who wore you down until you couldn't say no? Which date are you more likely to walk into with a positive outlook? Which person are you more likely to forgive for a little mistake or imperfection?

If you have to convince someone to work with you, chances are high that they'll have a bad attitude, unreasonable expectations, and little mercy. Your relationship with them is weak from the get-go. After the hard work of convincing them to hire you, you'll have an even harder time convincing them to trust and respect you. When you hit the bumps that are inevitable in every real estate transaction, you'll be the one feeling the pain.

Marketing guru Joe Polish calls those clients HALFs®: hard, annoying, lame, and frustrating. (The *L* could stand for lucrative, which these clients sometimes are, but that money is hard earned indeed.)

THE FAVORITE OR THE FOOL
THE FAVORITE OR THE FOOL

---

## The Connected:
## Joe Polish & Genius Network

Joe Polish is one of the most connected people on earth and the founder of Genius Network, a phenomenal network of entrepreneurs. Check it out at www.geniusnetwork.com.

---

When you're the Fool, life is rough.

## THE NEW WAY:
## HIGH-PROBABILITY ACTIVITY

Fortunately, the solution is simple: find out whether you're the Favorite or the Fool as fast as possible, and if you're not the Favorite, *walk away*. You're probably thinking that sounds incredibly scary, but bear with me.

There are two kinds of phone calls you'll get in your business. One is, "We're gonna sell, and we want you to list our home." The other is, "We're interviewing agents."

**Build your business around the first call.**

This is about stacking the odds in your favor. As Chris says, we live in a Las Vegas world, and not all the games give you the same chance of success. That first call is a table where your odds of winning are 80 percent. At the other table, your odds are just 20 percent. Which table do you want to sit at?

The answer seems obvious, but in reality, you've probably spent most of your career at that low-probability table: chasing and convincing, chasing and convincing, over and over, hoping and praying that someone will eventually pick you. You've seen how well that works. This book is about choosing to focus on high-probability activity instead. From now on, you're going to sit at the 80 percent table.

When you embrace the concept of the Favorite or the Fool, everything gets simplified. You no longer have to walk around on eggshells, worrying whether someone will work with you or not, fearful of saying or doing the wrong thing. When you're the Favorite, clients will commit to you up front, so there's no wondering or guessing. It's a magical thing.

When you do meet the prospective seller in their living room, it's not a listing appointment where you're trying to win them over with your valuable insights, which they may or may not swipe and use some other agent. Instead, it's a strategy meeting with paying clients who are already receptive to your advice. Building trust is natural, the work is more enjoyable, and the bumps in the road are easier to handle.

As Joe Polish puts it, those clients are ELFs®: easy, lucrative, and fun.

Best of all, those clients are far more likely to hire you repeatedly and refer people to you. That's the key to building the strong, reliable, profitable business you're dreaming of. We all know that repeat and referral business is the true gold mine of real estate, and now you know why: because you're already the Favorite. The more often you're the Favorite, the more often you *will be* the Favorite in the future. It's a virtuous cycle with the power to transform your entire career and life. Repeat and referral business is the low hanging fruit in real estate. Stop making the rookie mistake of not nurturing relationships on a daily basis.

Now, here's the part you're not going to like. You're going to resist this with every fiber of your being because it goes against what you've always believed about how to succeed in business.

To make room for high-probability activity, you have to say *NO* to everything else. (Gently, of course—we'll get to that later in this chapter.)

That's right—I'm telling you to let all those other opportunities pass you by. Turn them down, even though you may have a 20 percent chance of converting. Let them go. Save yourself the time, money, and heartache. They weren't going to go well for you anyway.

The FOMO is going to kick in hard here, but you've got to fight past it. That fear is lying to you. It's saying there aren't enough opportunities where you're the Favorite, and if you start passing things up, you won't do enough deals. Your business will fail. You'll lose everything. You'll starve. *You'll die.*

This is the place where your mind actually goes. Be ready for it. If you don't believe me, pay close attention to your self-talk next time you're in a competitive situation. You'll be shocked at the nonsense that takes place in your head.

But no, you're not going to die.

It's just your limbic brain—home of the survival instinct—blowing things out of proportion. The idea of giving up opportunities feels like a threat, so your brain revs up your anxiety, preparing you to fight, fly, or freeze. This isn't a saber-toothed tiger lurking in the bushes, ready to kill you, but your brain can't tell the difference.

As hard as it is to believe, even if you are the Favorite with only one or two out of ten people, there is still an abundance of business to do. There is never a lack of opportunity, only a lack of awareness, focus, and effort. When you make being the Favorite your standard for doing business, this choice will compound to your advantage in ways you never dreamed possible.

We've seen this play out time after time among the agents we coach. Choosing high-probability activity over low-probability activity is one of the first changes they have to make, and for most, it's an extremely challenging transition. It feels like you're going to lose business, and you might remember from Chapter 1 that human beings fear loss twice as much as they desire equivalent gains.

The truth is, the only things my agents have lost are dead-end prospects and bad clients. What they gain is more time, more peace of mind, easier work, happier clients, and more repeat and referral business.

See? There's truly nothing to fear about refusing to play the Fool. Here's what you should really be afraid of: if you waste your time playing the Fool for everyone, you might miss the chance to be someone's Favorite.

## WHICH ONE ARE YOU?

It only takes one conversation to know if you're the Favorite or the Fool. Chris and I call this process *getting proof of life*, which is what hostage negotiators do first to make sure the other party isn't yanking their chain. But instead of finding out if the hostage is really there and still breathing, you want to know if there's truly a deal here, and if so, whether it's going to be with you.

It's a **cold read**, just like what I used to do on the football field. Before each game, we would study the scouting report on our opponents. We had to learn everything backwards and forwards: all their stats and tendencies based on the down, distance, formation, field position, and a number of other factors. Knowing what the other team was likely to do in any given situation helped stack the odds in our favor come gametime. Our ability to anticipate just by reading the situation in front of us could be the difference between making the play and not making the play.

## Tool: The Cold Read

Paying close attention to the other person's words, tone, and body language to recognize patterns and predict their future behavior.

It's no different when you're in front of a potential seller or buyer. The clues as to whether you are the Favorite or the Fool are right there. The question is, do you recognize them? Do you know what sellers say and do when you're the Favorite? What about when you're the Fool? Being able to read the situation correctly is the difference between spending your time wisely or foolishly.

Some call this intuition, but it's really just pattern recognition, and humans are hardwired to excel at it. You have this ability already—you just need to hone it. Prospects act one way when you're the Favorite, another when you're the Fool. The more you practice reading these patterns, the easier it will be to tell the difference.

The following five questions will give you a solid framework to figure out whether you're the Favorite or Fool with each prospect. To be clear, these are questions you're asking *yourself*, not the prospect. *Don't* ask them these questions directly—we'll explain exactly what to say to get to the answers, using the Black Swan Method.[8] You'll see how prospects reveal the answers in the way they talk with you. The more confirmations you get, the more likely you're the Favorite.

## 1. Are they calling me specifically (or just agents)?

When talking to a prospect, the temptation is to jump straight into the sell. You want to tell them why they should work with you, why you could do the best job helping them sell or buy a home.

Don't. Instead, ask *them* to tell *you* why they want to work with you.

This is the first application of a principle that will come back later in the book: it matters who says it. When you explain why you're the right person for the job, you're convincing. When you let them explain it, you're putting their needs first and respecting their autonomy (which, as you learned in Chapter 1, people will die over).

---

[8] Developed by Chris Voss and his team at The Black Swan Group, www.blackswanltd.com.

So, ask the question: "I'm curious—of all the agents you know, why me?"

Tone of voice and pacing is critical. Go slow and be genuinely curious. Practice this line over and over again. Record yourself.

Now, listen to their answer...*without* hope in your heart. Don't think about what you're hoping to hear—just listen to what you're *actually* hearing. Are the reasons specific? Do they know who you are, or did they just call on a whim after seeing your number on a lawn sign or in a Google search result?

Their answer to this question tells you exactly how they view your value proposition. The more they know about you and can articulate their reasons for calling you specifically (not just any agent), the more likely you're the Favorite. A real answer is something you can label, mirror, and paraphrase.

Vague answers are a clue that you're the Fool in the game. They might even turn the question around on you and say, "You tell me why I should hire you." That's a big, waving red flag.

The "Why me?" question is so powerful that we have yet to see it fail to reveal whether an agent is the Favorite or the Fool. This is the prospect's chance to defend why they want to hire you. If you're the Favorite, they'll tell you. If you're not, they'll evade the question.

## 2. Do I fit the profile?

Here comes another throwback to Chapter 1: the best predictor of future behavior is past behavior. If they've ever bought or sold a home before, how did they pick their agent then? Was it based on a referral? Testimonials? Company affiliation? Some other factor?

Finding out how people have made big decisions in the past will help you understand how they are likely to choose an agent. There is probably a profile of the type of person that works best for them, and you want to evaluate whether you're a good match. For example, if they found their last agent through a personal connection, and you're a total stranger, the chances that they'll go with you are slim. The better you fit the profile, the more likely you're the Favorite.

Hint: If they have worked with another real estate agent in the past, be sure to find out whether they plan on working with that agent again. Instead of simply asking if they will, ask why they *wouldn't*: "Why would you not use the agent you worked with before?"

Here are some other questions you can ask to help clarify the profile:

What do you want in an agent?
How have you made decisions like this in the past?
How will you know when you've met the right person?
What guidance are you getting on this decision?
How do you see this process unfolding?

Again, listen carefully to their answers without fear and hope. Do you fit the profile of the agent they're looking for?

### 3. Can I make an emotional connection?

Now, can you get inside their head and read their mind? What you're looking for here is a "that's right" response.

Not "you're right," but *"that's right."*

We call that a two-millimeter shift: the difference seems small on the surface, but the consequences are massive. "You're right" is what someone says when they're caving to persuasion, or giving you a polite no or a false yes. "That's right" is what they say when they feel understood, which is the ultimate goal of everything in this book.

> ## Two-millimeter Shift:
> ## "You're right" ➜ "That's right"
>
> "You're right" means they feel defensive and resistant. "That's right" means they feel understood.

To get to "that's right," you'll use two essential tools from the Tactical Empathy toolbox: labeling and mirroring.

**Labeling** is stating what the other person is thinking, feeling, or doing—putting a label on it. A label starts with one of these phrases:

It sounds like...

It seems like...

It feels like...

You're probably thinking...

You're probably feeling...

It ends with your best guess about what they're actually thinking and feeling. You want to get inside the other person's head and heart, to see the world from their perspective. That requires deep listening. You can't be thinking about what you are going to say next. Your full attention needs to focus on the other person and where they're coming from.

---

## Tool: Labeling

Stating what the other person is thinking, feeling, or doing, using a phrase like "It seems like..." or "You're probably thinking/feeling..."

---

To them, your labeling feels like mindreading, and that builds trust. When you can clearly articulate what someone is thinking and feeling, they'll be much more open in their communications because they hear you "get it." This concept will come back again in future chapters.

Here are a few examples of labeling with a potential client:

It sounds like you have a very specific price in mind...

It seems like selling in a timely fashion is very important to you...

It feels like this is going to be a very emotional process for you...

You're probably thinking that your home will sell very quickly...

You're probably feeling frustrated with the number of showings on your property so far...

The interesting thing about labeling is that it doesn't matter if your label is right. If it is, you'll probably get "that's right" from the other person.

If it's not, they won't be annoyed. They'll just give you more information to correct your misinterpretation. In fact, intentional mislabeling can be a very effective way to get someone to reveal more. People love to correct you when your label is wrong—for them, fixing it feels good.

**Mirroring** goes hand in hand with labeling. To do it, just repeat the last few words the other person just said.

Seller: We want to sell our home quickly.

Mirror: Quickly?

Seller: Yes, we want to be sold and closed by the end of summer.

Mirror: End of summer?

Mirroring gives you more clarity on what someone is saying. It takes the place of just guessing, or saying something like "Tell me more," or "Can you be more specific?" It's a powerful tool for getting people to express their thoughts and feelings more fully.

---

## Tool: Mirroring

Repeating the last few words the other person just said, which often prompts them to expand on that train of thought.

---

Warning: Mirroring can feel very awkward at first. You'll probably feel like you're mimicking. Push past the discomfort and you'll quickly see the value of this tool. The more people open up and share, the more trust you create.

With both labels and mirrors, there's another two-millimeter shift going on: **"I" to "you."**

Most agents are constantly in "I" mode, making every conversation about what *they* think and feel. See for yourself—record and listen back to your client calls. Check your emails. It's "I," "I," "I" all over the place...but your interactions with clients and prospects are not about *you*. When you use "I," the other party is tuning you out.

Labels and mirrors shift you into "you" mode. They force you to concentrate on what the *other person* is thinking and feeling. To use these tools successfully, with the right tone and pacing, you have to come from a place of curiosity about the other person, not your own hope and fear. Suddenly, you're no longer talking about yourself and trying to steer the conversation in the direction you want. Instead, you're listening to them and talking about their concerns, needs, and desires.

---

### Two-millimeter Shift:
### "I" ➔ "You"

When you're using "I," you're focused on yourself. Use labels and mirrors to shift your attention back to the other person.

---

People can't hear you until they feel heard. They won't understand you until they feel understood. That's Tactical Empathy 101, the fundamental stuff that no one has taught you before. When you actually start doing it, it's money in the bank.

If you can use these tools to make the other person feel understood, you've created an emotional connection, and that's a very good sign that you might be the Favorite.

### 4. Is the conversation collaborative?

Another good sign is when the conversation is two-way—both you and the prospect are giving and receiving information. The opposite of this is the classic "picking your brain" scenario, when they call to get information out of you and aren't willing to give any in return.

The pricing conversation is the best example of this. If you say, "It sounds like you have a specific price in mind," and they answer you directly, that's a good sign that you're the Favorite because they're not afraid to share information with you.

If you're the Fool, they'll keep their cards close. They'll say, "I don't know. You're the expert. That's why we're calling you."

How annoying is that response? It's total nonsense. You know it and they know it. Every seller has a price in mind. They might not know if it's realistic, but it's there.

In this case, the most effective label for getting them to open up is: "It sounds like you have a very specific number in mind." If they still want to be evasive, try these:

You probably have looked on Zillow...
  Zillow shows a price of $_____ ...
  You probably think that's low...
  You're probably thinking closer to $_____ ... (Here you give
a much higher price, which will trigger the seller to say, "No, not that
much.")

The more you struggle to get straight answers about their target price
and other important pieces of information, the more likely you're the
Fool. When you're the Favorite, people will converse with you in an
honest way, and not be evasive or stingy with their responses.

## 5. Are they opposed to making a commitment up front?

This is the toughest part of this whole process. It's where the rubber
meets the road. You're going to think this will never work because
everyone around you is doing the exact opposite. You'll think that no
client in their right mind will agree to this.

Don't go see the property until the client has committed to working
with you.

I know, every other agent is willing to go out and give a listing presentation with no commitment whatsoever. They spend hours researching
the property and preparing for the appointment, then more hours
driving out there and having that conversation. All on spec, with no
assurance that they'll ever get anything in return.

Some call that selling, but we call it free consulting, and it's killing
your business. The more value you give away for free, the less valuable

THE FAVORITE OR THE FOOL

**The more value you give away for free, the less valuable you are.**

Why does someone need to work with you when you have given them your entire playbook at no charge? They have what they need, and will just go back to their Favorite to make sure they're doing all the things you suggested. How often does a seller take your price, or your staging suggestions, or your marketing ideas, and list with another agent? Would I be wrong to think this has happened more than once or twice in your career?

Plus, the more time and energy you waste on listing appointments you'll never win, the less you have for the people who actually want to work with you. So, *no more free consulting* (we'll come back to this in Chapter 4).

If you're the Favorite, getting a commitment won't be an issue. The prospect knows they want to work with you, and will gladly commit before seeing your analysis of the property because they trust your expertise.

If you're the Fool, you'll see that refusing to be the victim—declining to give the prospect valuable information for free—sometimes provokes an aggressive response. They might try to pressure you by saying things like "It sounds like you don't want my business." These attacks just reveal that person as a predator. Predators attack people who refuse to be victimized. If you think back to prospects who have given you a hard time, you'll recognize this behavior.

Don't take it personally, get upset, or let them sway you. Instead, exit the situation gracefully: "It sounds like you already have a few good agents to choose from. Why don't you meet with them, and if none of them work out, you can always reach out to me again."

## IT'S OKAY TO WALK AWAY

Everyone else is out there obsessing over their listing presentation, but the truth is, the whole thing is a farce. Sellers act like their minds are open, and they probably even believe it, but you know better now. They already had a Favorite before they even called you, and no listing presentation will change that.

I say it like it's obvious, but I know it's not. I spent the first twenty-five years of my coaching career teaching listing presentations. But when I found out (thanks to Chris) that it was all a waste of time, I changed my strategy in a heartbeat. In the five years since then, one truth has proven itself a million times over.

**It's not a sin to lose business—it's a sin to take a long time to lose business.**

Having a prospect get upset and walk away because you won't do a listing appointment is fine. Investing eight hours or more into a listing appointment and not getting hired is not fine. Convincing a client to hire you, and later walking away or getting fired because you couldn't meet their unreasonable demands is *not fine*.

That's why it's so important to answer all five of these questions in the very first conversation with each prospect. When you're just starting to practice this, it might take thirty minutes or even an hour to suss out whether you're the Favorite or the Fool. Over time, you'll get more and more efficient, until you can do it in under fifteen minutes.

Imagine that. Instead of wasting a whole day or more on each prospect and still having no idea what they'll do, you can spend just fifteen minutes finding out whether you have a serious shot or not.

That's life changing.

# KEY TAKEAWAYS

→ By the time prospects call you, you're either the Favorite or the Fool. Your only goal is to find out which one.

→ Develop your cold reading skills to spot patterns of behavior that indicate you're the Favorite. Your chances are high if:

  ▷ they called you specifically and can articulate why,

  ▷ you fit the profile of people they've worked with before,

  ▷ you connect emotionally with them,

  ▷ it's a two-way conversation, and

  ▷ they're willing to commit up front to working with you.

→ Only play at the table where the odds are in your favor. If you're the Fool, walk away gracefully before you waste any more time.

## Tactical Empathy Toolbox

→ **Cold Reading:** Paying close attention to the other person's words, tone, and body language to recognize patterns and predict their future behavior.

→ **Labeling:** Stating what the other person is thinking or feeling, using a phrase like "It seems like..." or "You're probably thinking/feeling..."

→ **Mirroring:** Repeating the last few words the other person just said, which often prompts them to expand on that train of thought.

Chapter 3

# NO MORE FREE CONSULTING

---

*Your only real value is the trust*
*you build with a client.*

---

IF YOU HAD HBO IN THE EARLY 2000s, YOU MIGHT HAVE WATCHED a show called Entourage, which revolved around an up-and-coming actor, Vincent Chase (played by Adrian Grenier), and his troublemaking friends.

Early in the series, Vincent goes looking for an agent to represent him in Hollywood. When he sits down in the first presentation, the agent shows a video that flashes one massive brand name after another: "Mercedes... Coca Cola...Vincent Chase. We intend to make you as popular as both of them." He's impressed.

At the next agency, he sits down, and it's the same thing. "Apple... Cannon...Vincent Chase." Vinny raises his eyebrows at his friend, clearly thinking, *This is the same thing we just sat through.*

At the third agency, it's the same spiel again: "Microsoft...McDonald's ...Vincent Chase...brand name recognition. What do you think?" This time, Vinny just walks out.

This is exactly what happens in the real estate industry.

Agents obsess over their listing presentations. They think that's how they win clients, so they pour effort into making their presentation marginally better than the next agent's. If you're focused on convincing prospects to choose you with facts, logic, and reason, the only way to differentiate yourself is to pack in more information and insight than anyone else. You give your time and value for free, hoping it will make you attractive enough for them to decide to pay you.

Agents call this a best practice, but they're kidding themselves. It's only a common practice masquerading as something more. Just because everyone else is jumping off a cliff doesn't make it a good idea.

You already know the logistical problems with this strategy. It takes hours, sometimes days, to do all the work involved in preparing, delivering, and following up on a listing presentation. If you don't get the job, that's a *lot* of wasted time. Plus, it's all too easy for the prospect to simply hand your playbook to the agent they wanted to work with in the first place. Your so-called competitive advantage is impossible to protect when you give it away like that.

And even with all that work, how is your listing presentation really any different from those of your top competitors? Are there any big secrets to the process of selling a home? I've sat in on hundreds of listing presentations, and while the style can vary, the substance rarely does. Real estate isn't rocket science. You can't set yourself apart with your pricing or staging or marketing tactics because everyone with a lick of sense will do it pretty much the same way.

The truth is, there's only one way to create a competitive advantage that's effective and lasting, and it has nothing to do with your value. None of the things you can put down on paper as reasons you're better than the next agent play into this. It's not about what you do but *how* you do it.

The only real way to differentiate yourself is with trust.

Trust is what makes a person choose you. It's what opens their mind to your influence, and it's what allows them to handle the bumps in the road without blaming you for every pothole. It's what leads to deals that feel good, even when they're not exactly what the client imagined at the beginning of the process. It's what makes them come back to you in the future, and refer other people to you. It's the foundation of a real estate business that's not just successful—it's sustainable.

In this chapter, you'll learn why trust is so much more powerful than value, and how to start building it from the very first moment you meet a prospect. It will go against every instinct you have as a salesperson... but *with* every instinct you have as a human being.

## THE OLD WAY: EXPLAIN YOUR VALUE

Every salesperson gets trained to define the value of their products and services for their customers. It makes perfect sense—before someone will give you money for something, they need to understand how it will benefit them.

You know it's true because you shop that way. When you're comparing yogurt brands in the grocery store, or deciding whether to shell out thousands for an elite professional development course, you look for those indications of value. Which one is better? Is it worth the money?

So, when you're selling your services, you try to communicate what makes *you* better than the others and worth the money. You talk about your track record, your market insight, your pricing strategy, your resources, your connections, your time commitment, and of course, your discounted fee. Maybe you deeply believe these things bring better results to your clients than what other agents can offer.

You say all this imagining the prospect will do some kind of mental math to figure out which agent will get them the best results. That's what a logical, reasonable person would do, right?

There's just one problem. To do that, they would have to take everything you say on faith. Even if what you claim is objectively true in your mind, your prospects can't possibly have the knowledge or experience to verify that. And, just because you sell a ton of homes doesn't mean working with you will be a good experience for them. Bottom line, they have no idea if you'll actually do the things you promise, or if they'll work.

There's simply no way to know in advance which agent will get them the best results. Choosing a real estate agent isn't like buying a laptop. With a laptop, you can look at the specs and try the machines for a few minutes to get a very accurate idea of which one will work best for you.

Not so with a real estate agent—you're, as the economists put it, an experiential product. It's impossible to know the benefits of working with you without actually working with you. Not only can prospects not know ahead of time which agent will be best, but they will *never* know for sure which would have been best, not even after the deal is done. They can't go back in time and see what would have happened if they had sold the same house under the same conditions with a different agent.

So, based on your value, you're indistinguishable from other agents—you're a commodity. And you know what commodities compete on? Price.

Of all the factors that make up your value as you've presented it to your prospects, the only one they can understand and verify is your fee. So, that ends up being what they focus on, even if you know it's not the biggest factor in how much money they'll take home when the deal is done. Competing on price isn't a sustainable way to run your business because there's always someone out there who will work for less or promise more.

Most agents I meet are stuck deep in this way of doing business, commoditizing themselves by focusing on articulating their value in the listing presentation. Occasionally, though, I'll find someone who relies on the force of their personality rather than the content of the listing presentation to win clients. They think that what truly sets them apart from other agents is *them*—their personality and how they interact with their clients.

That's getting closer to the truth.

## THE NEW WAY: BUILD TRUST

*You can't overcome emotion with fact, logic, and reason.*

Remember that, from the very beginning of this book? People make decisions based on emotions. Fact, logic, and reason are how they justify the decision after the fact. When it's impossible for a prospect to know your objective value, all they have left to go on is how they *feel* about you.

Don't forget, they're putting the biggest financial transaction of their lives in your hands. So, when I say "how they feel," it's not about whether they'd want to have a drink with you or be your friend. It's about whether they believe in your competence, honesty, and reliability. They want to know if they can *trust you* to make this a good experience for them.

**Your only real value is the trust you build with a client.**

Buying or selling a home is a stressful, emotional transaction, and there will be bumps in the road. Your clients will forgive you for those and let you guide them only if they trust you to protect their interests.

When they do, every aspect of the relationship works better. You can be more transparent with each other, collaborate more effectively, and get things done faster. They'll worry and nag you less, and you'll bring a more positive attitude to every interaction. The process won't be miraculously problem free, but each problem will feel more solvable and less stressful for both you and your client.

When you do a listing presentation the usual way, it does nothing to build that trust. You're just explaining about yourself and what you plan to do, not getting to know the other person and making them feel understood. Not building a relationship.

NO MORE FREE CONSULTING

---

### Two-millimeter Shift:
### Value ➜ Trust

When you sell your value, you become a commodity engaged in transactions. When you cultivate trust, you build relationships that lead to successful deals, repeat business, and referrals.

---

Let's be clear: I'm not talking about cultivating trust as a tactic to win over prospects. Remember from the last chapter, there's no winning anyone over. By the time they call you, you're already the Favorite or the Fool. Their mind is made up. This chapter is not—I repeat, *not*—about swapping building trust for explaining value as a method of convincing someone to choose you.

It's about *no longer trying to convince anyone at all.*

If you're the Favorite, focusing on trust from the get-go starts the relationship off on the right foot. If you're the Fool, it leaves them with a positive feeling about you, so they'll be inclined to speak highly of you, and even come back to you if things don't work out with their Favorite. It cannot magically turn you from the Fool into the Favorite—nothing can, and the whole point of the concept is that you shouldn't try.

That said, let's talk about how to build trust.

## THE INDIRECT ROUTE IS FASTER

Trust develops over time. You know this instinctively because you've built trust before. Look at all the people you trust in your life—did any of them gain that status instantaneously? Of course not. Trust builds incrementally over many conversations and shared experiences in which the other person repeatedly shows that they understand you, care about you, and will protect your interests.

That gradual process forces you to change your orientation as an agent. Instead of prioritizing short-term results, you have to focus on the long-term process. Instead of making yourself a commodity, you have to be a human being. Instead of convincing someone, you have to let them choose.

This is the indirect route.

It feels less efficient. It seems like it will take longer. But, it's like taking the ring road around a city instead of plowing through downtown traffic—less direct but much more effective. When you take the time to build trust first, everything that follows will be better and easier.

**The key to building trust is letting go of your feelings and desires.**

Your anxiety about whether they like you...your frustration that they're not listening to you...your hope for a smooth sale and a healthy commission...all that, and whatever other inner feelings and desires are yammering for your attention, has to go. Detach yourself from the outcome.

It's hard at first. We're all used to hearing and following that inner voice all day long. *I want this. I don't want that. I like this. I dislike that. I wish...I fear...I hope...*blah, blah, blah.

That voice is the roadblock to trust, and it's going to take some effort to learn to ignore it. Once you do, though, you'll never want to go back. You'll look back at your old, self-interested tactics, and they'll feel so dirty.

---

### Two-millimeter Shift:
### Controlling ➜ Letting Go

Talking is for chasing and convincing. Listening is for building trust. The way you listen has much more impact than anything you say or do.

---

It took a painful loss and some massively high stakes for me to learn to detach myself from the outcome. I wasn't drafted into the NFL—I was a free agent, and my only chance at getting signed was to go to training camp with the Miami Dolphins and hope I made the cut. They brought in ninety guys, and had to narrow the field to forty-five by the end of camp.

We practiced twice a day, and I was lucky if I'd get in four plays in an entire day. When the preseason games came, though, I got to play a lot, and I excelled. When the time came for the last cut, I did the math, and thought I had it made...but I was wrong. I was one of the very last cuts.

To get that close to my childhood dream and have it slip away was like having my heart ripped out and stomped on. I went back to my hotel room after being cut, closed the drapes, and sat in the dark having a pity party while I listened to the celebration of the guys who made the team. Pretty sad stuff.

Then, a miracle happened. The next day, I got a knock on my door. One of the forty-five final players was put on injured reserve, so a roster spot had opened up, and I was back on the team.

But in those twenty-four hours of misery, all my confidence and bravado had gone out the window. Now, I simply didn't want to make a mistake and get cut again. I knew what it felt like to lose my dream, and I was *not* going to let it happen a second time.

So, for the first five games of the season, I was no longer playing with reckless abandon, as I had done in the preseason. Now I was playing it safe, not taking risks and not putting myself out there. I was too worried about being cut again.

Before the sixth game of the season, I got a real wake up call. We were playing the New York Jets that week, and as I walked out to practice, Coach Shula was right in front of me. He spun around, looked me square in the eye, and said, "Son, you are not doing what we put you on this team to do." Then, he turned back and walked away.

The message was obvious: I was about to get cut again. In that moment, I made a life-changing choice. I stopped in my tracks, got very quiet, and decided I was going to give my best effort and let the outcome be whatever it was going to be.

If my best effort was good enough to keep my spot on the team, great.

If not, that would be okay too. Either way, my intent and focus was crystal clear: give my best effort, and don't be attached to the outcome. This moment has never left me, and this lesson has proven invaluable, as it will for you if you choose to learn from it.

Go out every day and give your best effort, and let the score take care of itself.

Most of us run around every day grasping for control over all the things we think are happening to us. News flash: life isn't happening to you. It's just happening. You're not in control of what happens, only of how you experience it.

Agents tear themselves up all the time with the illusion that they have control. When they get the listing, they think they did something right, and when they don't, they think they did something wrong.

What if you stop trying to force the outcome you want, and just see what happens? That's where trust begins.

## IF YOU'RE EXPLAINING, YOU'RE LOSING

Something incredible happens when you detach from the outcome, and ignore that voice in your head that's constantly nattering about what you feel and desire: you make mental space for the other person, your client. You can finally focus your complete attention on them and listen, for real.

Most people—especially salespeople—are terrible listeners. You're distracted by thoughts of the spat you had with your kid this morning, or the never-ending list of things you need to get done. If your mind is actually on the conversation at hand, it's busy predicting what the other person will say next, or preparing your response. It's focused on how *you* can steer the conversation toward the goal *you* have in mind. At the first opportunity, you jump in to finish their sentence for them, answer a question, or express your viewpoint.

There's virtually no actual listening—as in, receiving and comprehending someone else's speech—happening at all.

I used to be guilty of this too. I spent years developing scripts that were designed to lead a prospect or client neatly to the conclusion the agent wanted them to come to. Needless to say, the agent did most of the talking.

In fact, you were probably taught to believe that your value as an agent is in what you say: providing information, giving advice, and solving problems. So, you jump at the chance to speak because that's how you help your clients.

Except it's not.

On the contrary, it's impossible for you to help them until they trust you, and you build trust by *listening*, not talking. I'm not talking about some kind of fake "active listening" where you tell yourself to make eye contact, nod along, and say "I hear you" before launching into your own monologue. I mean real listening, the kind that only happens when you let go of what you want and focus exclusively on the other person.

We call that **proactive listening**—focusing *all* your attention on the other person, with the goal of seeing the world through their eyes. It's proactive in that you're watching for signs of negative emotions, and listening for ways to articulate your understanding of how they see the world. When you listen like that, you may very well make eye contact and nod along, but it's not about those outward signs—it's about what's going on in your mind. Who are you thinking about, you or them? Are you climbing aboard their train of thought, or stuck on your own? Are you seeking to make them understand, or make them feel understood?

## Tool: Proactive listening

Focus all your attention on the other person, with the goal of seeing the world through their eyes and expressing that understanding.

The way you listen has much more impact on your prospects and clients than anything you say or do. Think about that for a moment. It goes against everything you think you know, doesn't it? But when you start to truly listen well, you'll see it's true.

## Two-millimeter Shift: Talking → Listening

Talking is for chasing and convincing. Listening is for building trust. The way you listen has much more impact than anything you say or do.

Listen...then process...then speak to confirm your understanding.

When you do speak, instead of responding with your views, use the Tactical Empathy tools you've already learned. Label, mirror, paraphrase—all these tools require you to listen first, and keep your attention on the other person. Mirror their words to see if they have more to say about an idea. Use a label to confirm your understanding and make them feel heard. Use a deliberate mislabel to get a clearer picture of what they're really thinking and feeling.

Most importantly, if you hear yourself explaining, STOP.

As Ronald Reagan said, "If you're explaining, you're losing."

How often in a sales situation do you feel the need to explain or defend yourself? Why?

Explaining is the opposite of listening. It's a sign that you're focused on you again, and you don't build trust by focusing on yourself. It's also what you do when you're trying to convince someone of something, and remember, you're here to *find out* what's on their mind, not change it. They're not open to your influence until they trust you—until you make them feel understood.

## BEND THEIR REALITY

I know what you're thinking...but what if you need to change their mind? What if they're about to make a decision they'll regret because they aren't seeing something clearly?

First of all, tread carefully here. You are not the authority on what your client wants or what is good for them. They are. Your role is not to

NO MORE FREE CONSULTING

help them decide what they want—it's only to provide enough information for them to do that themselves. Please take all your superhero capes and put them back in the closet where they belong. You don't need to save anyone from themselves. That is not your job as a real estate professional.

Remember the analogy about standing on the opposite side of the road from your client? First, you have to cross to their side and stand shoulder to shoulder with them. Then, you look at what they're seeing and where they want to go. Finally, you help them navigate the path to their destination.

In that process, there are moments when you, as an expert on the local neighborhood, will have information your client doesn't. Maybe they want to go to the top of a mountain off in the distance, but have no idea of the danger, time, or cost involved. Or maybe they want to cross to the other side of a field, but they don't know there's a marsh in the middle, and it would be easier to go around the field instead of straight through.

Let's stick with that analogy for a moment. Imagine your client wants to go to the top of a huge mountain off in the distance. They're thinking of the stunning view they'll have from up there, and if you suggest that it would be much easier and almost as good to climb a nearby hill instead, all they will see is the loss: a nice view instead of a magnificent one. Not an attractive proposition.

What they don't know (and you do) is that to get up that mountain, they'll have to cross a desert, then climb a rock face, then hike through knee-deep snow in gale-force winds. It will be dangerous, expensive, and take weeks. On the other hand, they can walk up that local hill in an afternoon.

You can't change their mind—only they can. And because fear of loss is the primary motivator of human beings (see Chapter 1), they'll do that if they perceive their previous choice as a greater loss than some other option. In this case, the client was focused on the loss of that magnificent view...but you can bring to their attention the loss of time and money and possibly life it would take to get it. Then, they can decide which loss is worse.

Chris calls this a **focused comparison**. You're not changing the facts of reality. You're just changing how the other person perceives them—*bending* their reality, if you will.

This happens all the time with home pricing. Sellers are notorious for having inflated views of the value of their homes, and they often have their hearts set on an asking price that will prevent the house from selling quickly. When you suggest they lower the price, all they perceive is the loss (of money they never had in the first place, but it doesn't matter —it still feels like a loss). What they're not thinking about is the loss of time when the house goes unsold for six months, or how much more they might have to reduce the price by that point.

> ## Tool: Focused comparison
>
> Framing the facts to focus the other person's attention on the potential losses associated with each option they face. Comparing potential losses instead of gains often changes how they think about the decision.

You can't change their mind. You can't *convince* them to lower the price, and to try would only undermine their trust in you. The only thing you can do is bend their reality. Give them a full, accurate picture of the potential losses they face with each option...and let them choose.

For example, here are several different ways to phrase the situation.

On the one hand, you want to make sure you are not going to leave any money on the table. On the other hand, you want to make sure your home sells. What pricing strategy makes more sense to you: pricing the home so the buyer is looking at what they love about the home, or pricing it so the buyer is looking at what they don't like?

Or:

You obviously want to sell your home for the most money possible. What do you think is the better pricing strategy: making the buyers reach for your price, or creating a bidding war where buyers are competing against each other for your home?

Or:

You have a number in your head that makes sense to you. Anything less would feel like a loss. The question is, what is the best way to get the result you want without jeopardizing the sale because you listed the home at a price that scared potential buyers away?

Or:

Here is what you are up against if you price your home at that number... As crazy as it sounds given this hot market, while it is almost impossible to price a home too low, it is still very possible to price a home too high. That doesn't make much sense, does it? What concerns, if any, do you have about overpricing your home so that it sits and doesn't sell...causing you to miss out on this market altogether?

Once again, it's not about you. You're here to find out what your client really wants, and help them get it. Your feelings and desires have no place in that process, and they'll only get in your way.

## HOW YOU DO BUSINESS

At first glance, it's hard to believe that letting go of your desires will help you achieve them. How on earth are you going to get more clients and more income if you *stop* trying to get them? It sounds crazy.

But here's the reality I've seen over and over in this industry: when agents do things the typical way, more business brings more stress. More money and status, maybe, but also worse quality of life, and less time to enjoy that money.

There's a reason agents have a terrible reputation. They allow themselves to be defined by their production level, so they turn into mercenaries chasing after blood money. They become addicted to more, which just creates higher expectations and more pressure in a never-ending, vicious cycle.

There's a high cost to doing business that way. Just like in my first five games with the Miami Dolphins, constantly pushing for what you want actually gets in the way of doing what it takes to get it. By focusing on your goals, you push away the people who will help you achieve them: your clients.

So, forget about convincing anybody of your value, or of anything else, for that matter. The only thing you need to do is build a trusting relationship...and the only way to do that is to detach from the outcome. Let go of your feelings and desires. Focus on making them feel truly understood, and everything else will fall into place.

Your primary job as a real estate agent is to cultivate relationships on a daily basis.

I want to repeat this in capital letters: YOUR PRIMARY JOB AS A REAL ESTATE AGENT IS TO CULTIVATE RELATIONSHIPS!

The consequences of this decision will ripple through your entire business and life. It starts with the Favorite or the Fool—that concept alone saves you countless hours of pitching to people who were never going to hire you in the first place. Now, when you build trust with your clients, every conversation, every hurdle, every decision is easier to navigate. It takes less time, feels better, and occupies less of your mental space. Your clients see you as a trusted advisor, and are more likely to follow your guidance and bring you more business in the future.

Trust doesn't just give you more time and money—it brings you joy and inner peace.

*That's* what we mean when we say that how you do business is more important than how much business you do.

This is what happens when you do business as an authentic human being with other human beings. You're not a commodity, and they're not paychecks. We're all here on earth to be of service to others, and you're learning how to find the people who want your help...and help them.

# KEY TAKEAWAYS

→ Explaining value is about fact, logic, and reason. Building trust is about emotion, connection, and relationships.

→ The first one seems easier, but it doesn't work because that's not how people really make decisions. Plus, it turns you into a commodity, because there's always someone who will promise more and charge less.

→ When you take the time to build trust first, everything that follows will be better and easier.

→ The key to building trust is letting go of your feelings and desires. That's what allows you to focus your complete attention on them, and truly listen.

→ You can't convince anyone to do anything, and to try only undermines their trust in you. Instead, influence them by bending their reality, i.e., focusing their attention on potential losses they hadn't previously considered. Then, preserve the trusting relationship by letting them make the decision.

### Tactical Empathy Toolbox

→ **Proactive Listening:** Focus all your attention on the other person, with the goal of seeing the world through their eyes.

→ **Focused Comparison:** Framing the facts to focus the other person's attention on the potential losses associated with each option they face. Comparing potential losses instead of gains often changes how they think about the decision.

Chapter 4

# GET THE ELEPHANTS
# OUT EARLY

*The reasons someone might **not** want to do
business with you are more important
than the reasons they do.*

AFTER NURTURING A POTENTIAL CLIENT FOR OVER FIVE YEARS,
Tracey* finally got the listing. The owner, Dave*[9], was ready and motivated
to sell, and Tracey would have been elated, but there was just one problem:
Dave's expectations were unrealistic.

He wanted to list at $1.5 million without doing any staging, and he
was convinced that his market research justified that price. Tracey knew
better, and she gently suggested that the price might be a little high, and
that staging was probably a good idea, but Dave wasn't interested. She

---

[9] Names have been changed.

figured she could either take the listing on his terms or lose it, and she wasn't about to give up on a prospect she had put so much effort into already.

So, they did what he wanted and waited to see who would bite... and waited, and waited some more. Weeks went by with no offers. No one even wanted to come see the house. It was clear that Dave's plan had been a bad idea.

Now, Tracey is in a tough spot. She can try to convince Dave to lower the price by $100K and invest $10K in staging, and if she succeeds, the house will probably sell quickly. That won't feel like a win to Dave, though. He'll think he lost $110K, and because a loss stings twice as much as an equivalent gain, he'll *feel* like he lost $220K. That's not the kind of emotion that leads to referrals.

If she fails to convince him, or if she doesn't try, the listing will expire. Another agent will come in, relist at a lower price, and get the commission, while Tracey walks away with nothing to show for all her effort.

She's between a rock and a hard place, and it's all because she didn't get the elephants out early.

She's not alone—the vast majority of agents do exactly what she did, and you probably do too. My coaching calls are full of problems just like this one: tough conversations that agents dread to have with their clients.

Pricing is a common sticking point, but it's far from the only one. Tough conversations happen throughout the process, from getting hired all the way to closing the deal. Anytime your client's desires and expectations don't match up with reality, you've got a tough conversation on your hands.

Depending on how you approach them, these conversations can build one of two things: trust or resentment. Unfortunately, our instincts tend to lead us down the second path instead of the first.

In this chapter, you'll learn why the usual way of addressing problems is so counterproductive, and how to do it in a way that strengthens your relationship with your clients instead of undermining it. Instead of treating tough conversations as threats, you'll see them as opportunities.

## THE OLD WAY: AVOID AND SUGARCOAT

No one likes to be the bearer of bad news. Bad news upsets people, and you don't want your clients to be upset—you want them to be happy. You want them to have confidence in you. You want them to *like* you.

Telling them something they don't want to hear doesn't seem like the best way to achieve that, does it? If you reveal the ugly truth, you might lose the client or the deal.

So, you try not to mention anything that might drive them away. When you're wooing them to hire you, you focus on why they should work with you, and avoid any hint of why they might not want to. That includes your commission—ideally, it never comes up until they see the contract, and then they just sign without questioning it, and you breathe a big sigh of relief.

When you're getting ready to list (or search for properties, if your client is a buyer), you prefer not to crush their dreams, even if you know their expectations are totally out of whack. They'll figure it out for themselves when they see that their house doesn't sell, or their budget won't get them everything they're hoping for. That way, reality is the one that disappoints them, not you.

Some ugly truths can't be avoided, though. When the inspection reveals problems, when the counteroffer gets rejected, when the other side is asking for concessions...you have to say something.

If you are like most agents, you dread these conversations. They're the ones that keep you up at night, imagining how your clients will explode at you, or maybe even fire you. It's the absolute worst part of your job, so you often find yourself delaying and searching for ways out of the situation. Standard practice is to take the problem, stick it in a drawer, and hope it goes away magically.

How much time have you spent spinning things in your head in an effort to preserve what you hope is the client's favorable opinion of you?

At some point in the transaction, though, you have to face the music. When that time comes, you play down the negatives and look for a silver lining or some kind of solution to the problem, hoping that might mitigate their anger and disappointment. As the saying goes, "Bring me solutions, not problems." If you do that, they can't fault you, right?

Whether you're avoiding or sugarcoating, minimizing your client's negative emotions is the name of the game.

I get it. If you're anything like most agents, you're a people person... dare I say, a people pleaser. You hate to upset anyone, and you hate even more for anyone to be upset *at you*. You know unhappy clients won't refer to you in the future, and they make you miserable in the present, so you do everything in your power to squash negativity.

Unfortunately, while avoiding and sugarcoating may seem to keep negative emotions at bay, what those tactics really do is generate stress and undermine your clients' trust in you. People may not like hearing bad news, but what they like even less is getting blindsided by it, and that's exactly what happens when you try to tiptoe around the tough stuff. When they finally see the problem, they think, *Why am I hearing this now when you could have told me ages ago?*

There are only two answers to that, and neither one makes you look good. The first is you didn't anticipate this problem, in which case your competence comes into question. The second is you did anticipate it, but didn't say anything, which makes them wonder what else you're holding back, and whose interests you're prioritizing—theirs or your own. The cover up is always worse than the crime.

Instead of protecting your relationship with your clients, avoiding and sugarcoating bad news has inadvertently wrecked it.

## THE NEW WAY: BE A STRAIGHT SHOOTER

Bad news is a bummer, but you know what everyone likes? A straight shooter: someone who tells it like it is, and doesn't keep you guessing or try to pull the wool over your eyes.

Instead of shying away from problems, a straight shooter confronts them head-on as soon as they become apparent, just like the buffalo in the storm. While this may seem scary, it always leads to better outcomes for both you and your client. If the problem is a dealbreaker for them, it's better to get it on the table now than to waste more of anyone's time on a deal that will never close. If it's not, they'll thank you for bringing it up as soon as possible.

Don't mistake this transparency for brutal honesty. We're in the business of making people feel understood, and brutality has no place there. There's no reason honesty has to feel like a brick to the face, and it never should if you're delivering it right.

That's what the rest of this chapter is about: how to deliver bad news and confront negative emotions in a way that makes people feel understood. You'll learn exactly what to say, how to say it, and why these nuances of language are such powerful tools for building trust with your clients.

## CALL OUT THE NEGATIVES

If you've been in an airport or on public transit recently, you've probably seen signs that say, "If you see something, say something." That's a Department of Homeland Security slogan urging you to report suspicious activity to law enforcement, but you might as well print that out and slap it on your office wall, because it applies to real estate too.

In fact, it applies to every kind of tough conversation, from family spats to hostage negotiations. It's one of the key negotiation tactics that Chris learned in his time with the FBI, and continues to use with all his negotiation coaching clients. Only instead of reporting suspicious activity, you're calling out negative emotions.

Whenever you sense that your client is unhappy, say so. It doesn't matter whether you know the reason why. It doesn't even matter if your interpretation of their mood is correct. If you see something, say something: "You seem upset/frustrated/disappointed," or whatever emotion fits best.

You probably think this sounds crazy. Why would you call attention to a negative emotion—isn't that just inviting it out to play? And what if you're just imagining it—wouldn't that just create a problem where there wasn't one?

Here's the truth: it's *impossible* to speak a problem into existence. If you're mistaken, they'll correct you, no harm done. If you're not, and there really are negative emotions happening, naming them actually reduces them.

That's science. Studies have shown that when people label their negative emotions, their physiological experience of those emotions diminishes.[10] All those stress symptoms that pop up when you're upset—elevated heart rate, shallow breathing, high blood pressure, sweating, nausea, muscle tension, etc.—actually get better when you put a label on what you're feeling. (Remember labels from Chapter 2? Yep, here they come again.)

Why does this work? It all comes back to Tactical Empathy, a.k.a. making people feel understood.

When someone tells you not to feel something (*Don't be upset!*), does that make you feel understood? Of course not. It does the opposite —it convinces you that they don't understand your perspective at all. Denying negative emotions has a 100 percent failure rate.

---

[10] Alex Korb, *The Upward Spiral: Using Neuroscience to Reverse the Course of Depression, One Small Change at a Time* (Oakland: New Harbinger Publications, 2015).

What about when they ignore what you're feeling? No, you don't feel understood then either. Once in a while, unspoken negative emotions just fade away, but most of the time, they fester like an untreated wound. Not pleasant.

You're probably starting to see why labeling negative emotions is the way to go. By calling them out instead of waiting for the other person to bring it up, you show that you're paying attention to how they feel. When they feel understood, their brains release oxytocin, which mitigates the stress response. Your label doesn't fan the flames of negativity—it douses them.

This works even if the label is completely wrong. If you say, "You seem upset," when they're not, they won't hesitate to say, "No, I'm just thinking through my options," or whatever else is going on in their heads. As we mentioned in Chapter 2, a mislabel often leads the other person to reveal even more information than a correct label does. And it still makes them feel understood, because you've shown your consideration for their feelings, and given them an opportunity to communicate their thinking.

## GET IN FRONT OF THINGS

The fear of speaking problems to life also keeps agents from preparing their clients for what lies ahead. Before you ever talk to a prospective client, you already know about all the objections they might have to working with you, not to mention all the obstacles they might face once the work begins. But if you're like most agents, you don't say anything. You just cross your fingers, and hope those issues won't come up.

That automatically puts you behind the ball. It sets you up for that ugly question: *Why didn't you tell me sooner?* Don't put yourself in that position. Instead, bring up those objections and obstacles before they take you down.

Once again, this might seem crazy. Why on earth would you talk about reasons not to work with you when your goal is to convince them to hire you? Why would you freak them out now about problems that may or may not come up during the sales process?

Because it builds trust.

## Two-millimeter Shift:
## Waiting ➜ Getting in Front of Things

When you delay the delivery of potentially negative information, you undermine the other person's trust in you. Instead, bring it up as soon as you can. If it's a dealbreaker, you waste less time, and if not, your transparency builds trust.

Not long ago, Chris was shopping for a new car. At the dealership, he asked the salesman if the chassis of the car he was looking at was good. "Of course!" the salesman said. "It's the best on the market!"

Would you have believed that guy? Yeah, neither did Chris.

Now, imagine the salesman had said something like, "Well, it's the best on the market for off-roading, but it's not the most comfortable for city driving and long road trips."

Suddenly, he seems like a trustworthy source of guidance for your car purchase. And look at how he did it—by anticipating a possible objection. Instead of pretending his product was perfect, he acknowledged up front that it wasn't ideal for everyone.

Could that cost him a sale? You might think so, but think again.

Would anyone who objected to a stiff ride have ever bought that car anyway? No, but they might have wasted another hour of the salesman's time before figuring out the car didn't meet their needs. Or worse, they might have bought the car and then brought it back a week later, having realized their mistake. Either way, the salesman would have been better off if the customer had walked away in the beginning.

That's why the reasons someone might *not* want to do business with you are more important than the reasons they do. You are not a trustworthy authority on your own value...unless you also acknowledge the client's potential objections. Then, instead of convincing the client to hire you, you're simply informing them and allowing them to choose for themselves. As we mentioned in Chapter 1, people will die over their autonomy. When you let them keep it, their trust in you grows.

## Two-millimeter Shift:
## Why ➜ Why Not

The reasons someone might *not* want to do business with you are more important than the reasons they do.

Warning people about potential obstacles achieves the same thing.

Just imagine your friend invites you to go for a walk in the park. Only when you arrive do you realize that it's a National Park, and the trail is several miles of hilly terrain. You're totally unprepared, and by the end, you're exhausted, dirty, sunburnt, bug-eaten, and dehydrated. Oh yeah, and angry at your friend.

Now, imagine that instead, she invites you on a long, challenging hike and advises you to wear sturdy shoes and bring water, sunscreen, bug spray, and a raincoat, just in case. It's the same trail as before, but in this scenario, you're ready for it. It's still a tough hike, but at the end, you're grateful for the advice she gave you, and happy you didn't even need to use the raincoat.

Preparing your clients for the possible challenges ahead won't scare them off—if it does, they weren't ready for this road anyway, and working with them was never going to end well. For the clients that *are* ready, discussing potential issues before they arise can only build their confidence in you. It shows you know what you're doing and want them to have the best possible experience. If any of those problems come to pass, they'll be thankful for the advance warning, and if nothing bad happens, they'll be even happier that you were able to smooth the road for them.

## BRACE THEM FOR BAD NEWS

In this business, there's no escaping bad news. No matter how well you do your job, problems happen. Sometimes they're outside your control, and sometimes they're not. Sometimes you anticipated them and warned your client, and sometimes you didn't. Regardless, you have to deliver the message.

The good news is that people want you to tell them the truth... gently. Don't just blurt it out, but don't dance around it either. Instead, ease them into it with two powerful techniques: bracing and the Accusations Audit.

**Bracing** is deceptively simple: "I have some bad news."

Those five words give you the ability to have any tough conversation. They instantly make it easier for both you and your client to broach any uncomfortable subject.

> ## Tool: Bracing for Bad News
>
> Before you deliver potentially negative information, prepare the other person by saying, "I have some bad news."

This is one of the most important and valuable phrases you will learn in this book. "I have some bad news..." is such an incredibly versatile turn of words, and can be used in so many different situations. Once you get comfortable with this language, you will never fear another difficult conversation. It gives you a way in whenever there is something challenging that needs to be discussed.

These words inspire dread, which is, unbelievably, the point. When you say them to a client or prospect or agent, the first place their mind goes is death—literally.

*Bad news? What could it possibly be?* In a fraction of a second, they're already picturing the most horrifying thing they can think of.

That's the beauty of it: the actual bad news is almost never as bad as they imagined. Instead of going from neutral to upset, they're going from terrified to upset, which actually feels like a *relief*. The facts of the situation are no different, but they feel less terrible than they would have if you hadn't braced them.

---

### Two-millimeter Shift:
### Sugarcoating ➡ Bracing

When you try to put a positive spin on bad news, it comes across as disingenuous and manipulative. Bracing them for it softens the blow.

---

There's a second reason this works so well. The regions of the brain that react to emotional pain are the same as those for physical pain, and studies of physical pain show that bracing for it can actually reduce the perceived intensity of the pain. If you say, "This is gonna hurt," the person prepares mentally, and if the blow strikes within a short window after that, it hurts less than if it had struck without warning. You can't wait too long, though, or the anticipation itself becomes painful.

So warn them, wait for them to give you permission to proceed, then let it fly. This concept is one of the easiest things to implement in this whole book, and it instantly transforms your approach to tough conversations.

## DO AN ACCUSATIONS AUDIT

You can take this even further—and we strongly recommend that you do—with an **Accusations Audit**. When you anticipate that a client (or anyone else) will have a very negative reaction to your news, this is an essential tool for reducing the fallout.

The essence of it is this: before you deliver the bad news, you tell your client all the horrible things they'll think and feel when they hear it. You lay out all the possible accusations they might make, no holds barred (which is why it's called an Accusations Audit). You keep going with the accusations until the client pushes back, and *only then* do you deliver the news.

## Tool: Accusations Audit

To defuse potential negative emotions, articulate all the awful things the other person might think or feel in response to your message.

The easiest way to understand this is to see it in action. So, let's go back to the story of Tracey and Dave from the beginning of the chapter. Tracey has to tell Dave that the house won't sell unless he lowers the price and invests in staging. If she's savvy enough to use bracing and the Accusations Audit, here's how that conversation would go.

Tracey: "Dave, I have some bad news."

*That's bracing. She's asking permission to deliver the truth.*

Dave: "Uh oh. What's going on?"

*She just got the go-ahead signal.*

Tracey: "You're not going to want to hear this. You're going to be furious. You'll think I have no idea what I'm doing. You might even want to fire me."

*With these accusations, Dave starts to wonder what could possibly be so bad.*

Dave: "What do you mean?"

Tracey: "You're going to wonder why I didn't say this before. You'll probably question my intentions, and think I deceived you in some way."

THE FULL FEE AGENT

*The more extreme the accusation, the more Dave wants to distance himself from it. He wants to think of himself as a reasonable person, not someone who would think or say those things.*

Dave: "I wouldn't think that, Tracey."

*He pushes back on the accusations, giving Tracey the signal that it's safe to deliver her message.*

Tracey: "The reality is, this house won't sell unless we get it professionally staged and lower the price by $100K."

*She delivers the news clearly, without sugarcoating, apologizing, taking responsibility for the situation, or trying to solve it. She simply states the facts, then waits in complete and total silence.*

Dave: "Wow. Okay. I appreciate your honesty. That's a tough pill to swallow, but I guess we have to do what we have to do. Let me think about it overnight, and I will get back to you in the morning."

The next day, Dave might come back and say, "My wife and I talked this over. We've got to be realistic about this if we want it to sell. Let's do it. Lower the price and let's set up the staging."

What just happened? Why wasn't Dave upset after Tracey told him exactly what he didn't want to hear?

It's the same thing that happens with "I have some bad news," only more powerful. If you overblow the prospect of negativity, when you finally deliver the news, it feels like a relief. By verbalizing your client's worst possible reactions ahead of time, you actually inoculate against them. You take away their gunpowder.

It's simple, but counterintuitive. Put yourself in Dave's shoes. You like to think of yourself as a reasonable person, not someone who would explode with rage. You chose Tracey to help you, and don't want to think you put your trust in the wrong person. So, when she says, "You're going to want to fire me" and "You're going to think I deceived you," your instinct is to distance yourself from that. By saying those things, she made you want to *avoid* making them true.

> ## Two-millimeter Shift:
> ## Solving Problems ➜ Defusing
> ## Negative Emotions
>
> When problems come up, your instinct is to solve them, but that's not what your clients need. Instead, use an accusations audit to defuse their negative emotions so *they* can make an informed decision about how to proceed.

Notice that Tracey *kept going* with the accusations until Dave pushed back on them. That was the signal that he didn't want to think and feel those things, and had braced himself against them. At that point, he had decided to receive the news calmly, no matter how bad it was. That's when Tracey knew it was safe to proceed.

This pushback can manifest in different ways. Here are some of the things clients might say that signal they're ready to hear your message:

- I wouldn't think/say/do/feel that.
- You're being too hard on yourself.
- It can't be that bad.
- Just tell me already.
- Rip the bandaid off.

The more trust you've built with a client, the quicker this happens. When trust is weak, it can take a lot more accusations to get to this point. If their verbal or body language (including silence) in any way indicates they might agree with your accusations, you haven't gone far enough yet.

That's why it's important to prepare thoroughly for the conversation. Before you go into this situation, sit down and write out all the negative things the client could possibly think or feel in response to what you're going to tell them. Be specific. For example:

- You're going to be crushed/furious/disgusted/etc.
- You'll probably feel that I let you down.
- You're going to think I should have seen this coming.
- You'll probably wonder how this could happen when the market is so hot.
- You're going to think I was out of touch with the market.
- You'll probably think I'm only concerned about my own interests.
- You'll probably want to fire me on the spot.
- You'll think I'm the worst agent in the world.
- You're going to hate me.

Remember, it's impossible for a label to plant a negative thought that wasn't already there, so get as extreme as possible. There's no way to overdo it. The harsher the negative label is, the more likely your client will push back on it, which is exactly what you want.

As you prepare, you can also use the same strategy to reduce your own negative emotions. Just label all the negative things you're thinking and feeling as you anticipate the conversation. For example:

- I'm feeling fearful.
- I'm afraid the client will yell at me.
- I'm looking for a way to sugarcoat this.
- I'm looking for a way out of this conversation.
- I'm scared.

Another thing you should do to prepare is practice your **late night FM DJ voice**. Slow down and speak in a low, soothing tone, as if you were the host of a late night radio show. This tone is highly effective at getting other people to relax and slow down because calm is contagious.

---

### Tool: Late Night FM DJ Voice

A low, slow, soothing tone of voice that's highly effective at getting other people to relax and slow down.

---

Look back at Tracey and Dave's conversation. At any point, did she explain her thinking, defend herself, or debate with her client? No. She just laid out what she imagined Dave would be thinking and feeling, then delivered the truth. That's all you need to do. You don't need to solve the problem, or even explain how it happened. You just need to deliver the news gently, and that's exactly what the Accusations Audit allows you to do. It minimizes the negativity that both you *and* your client experience.

Sometimes, you don't get the chance to do an Accusations Audit before the bad news drops. Instead, your client finds out first, and then you have to deal with the aftermath. The Accusations Audit is still useful in that situation. All you have to do is adjust your phrasing: "You'll probably _____" becomes "You probably _____," and "You're going to _____" becomes "I know you _____."

Here's an insider tip from Chris: "I know" is the way to go when the other person is really upset. He started using "I know" instead of "You probably" when talking to the families of kidnapping victims. Imagine saying to the parents, "You're probably worried about your daughter's safety." *Probably?* It's insulting just to imply there might be a chance they're not. But you're not guessing—you *know* they're worried. So, say so.

## SILENCE IS YOUR FRIEND

Once you've delivered the news, there's one more thing you need to do: shut up.

Seriously. Just stop talking. Let there be **silence**. Don't try to fill it —the other person needs it. They need mental space to process what you've just said and consider their options, and if you keep speaking, you're stealing that from them.

Most people can't stand silence in a conversation. They think it means something is wrong, so it makes them feel extremely uncomfortable. The reflex is to fill it with anything you can think of—small talk, platitudes, questions, anything to keep it from being awkward.

But what if silence actually means something *good* is happening? What if it's an indicator that the other person is doing exactly what you need them to do: *thinking* about what you've just told them?

> ## Tool: Silence
>
> After you deliver your information, stop talking. Give the other person ample space to process what you've said and express themselves. Let them break the silence. It's not awkward— it's essential.

If you're like most agents, when you deliver bad news, or lay out a tough choice for your clients, you usually jump straight into problem solving. Instead of stepping back and giving the client room to think, you try to do the thinking for them, and it's not out of the goodness of your heart. It's out of fear. Maybe if you can solve the problem, the client won't get upset or blame you for it.

THE FULL FEE AGENT

But your problem solving is just getting in their way. How well would *you* think with someone jabbering at you nonstop?

Silence isn't just something you should learn to tolerate. It's a tool you need to use proactively in every tough conversation you have. Do your Accusations Audit, deliver the bad news, and be quiet. The last step is just as important as the first two.

In the next chapter, you'll see exactly why.

# KEY TAKEAWAYS

→ When you avoid tough conversations and sugarcoat bad news, you undermine your clients' trust in you, and their ability to make informed decisions.

→ Everyone likes a straight shooter—someone who tells the truth *gently*.

→ Don't beat around the bush or try to solve the problem for them. Just brace them for the bad news, and use an Accusations Audit to defuse their negative emotions.

→ Once you've delivered the news, be quiet. Silence gives the other person the space they need to process what you've said and consider their options.

## Tactical Empathy Toolbox

→ **Bracing for Bad News:** Before you deliver potentially negative information, prepare the other person by saying "I have some bad news."

→ **Accusations Audit:** To defuse potential negative emotions, articulate all the awful things the other person might think or feel in response to your message.

➡ **Late Night FM DJ Voice:** A low, slow, soothing tone of voice that's highly effective at getting other people to relax and slow down.

➡ **Silence:** After you deliver your information, stop talking. Give the other person ample space to process what you've said and express themselves. Let them break the silence. It's not awkward—it's essential.

Chapter 5

# PUT THE RESPONSIBILITY WHERE IT BELONGS

*Own your role as the trusted advisor.
It's not your job to decide anything—
only your client can do that.*

ONE OF MY COACHING CLIENTS, VICTORIA\*, HAD A FRIEND, JASMINE\*[11], who wanted to help her purchase a multimillion-dollar home. Jasmine wanted to work with someone she trusted, so she reached out to Victoria, who was thrilled at the prospect of working with her friend. While Jasmine's expectations seemed a little unrealistic, Victoria agreed to help her because she didn't want to disappoint her friend. You've all been in a similar situation.

---

[11] Names have been changed.

Unfortunately, Victoria's instincts were right. After several months of looking and writing offers and missing out on properties, both Victoria and Jasmine were feeling exhausted and frustrated, and there was some unspoken tension building between them. Victoria was disheartened because she felt like she was letting Jasmine down. In her mind she was responsible for getting Jasmine into a new home, and she was failing. This client relationship, which she had thought would be fun and easy, had actually created a massive amount of unnecessary work and anxiety in Victoria's life.

Don't blame the client, though. The agent is the one at fault here, but not for failing to get her friend into a new home. Her problem was strictly in her own head.

She was taking on responsibility for things that were outside her control.

She didn't control what her friend was willing to offer for a new home. The only thing under her control was making sure Jasmine saw the best properties and knew what it would take to complete a successful purchase, including price, terms, contingencies, timing, etc. She had no ability to make Jasmine pay more than what she wanted.

Victoria was putting herself through the emotional grinder day after day for something that wasn't her responsibility at all. Real estate agents do this to themselves all the time, and not just when the client is a friend. You think you should control every aspect of the process, so when something goes wrong, you think you're at fault—or if not at fault, at least responsible for solving the problem.

Here's the hard truth: you have no decision power in this process.

Your role is to be an advisor. It's not your job to decide anything—only your client can do that. All you can do is lay out the landscape and present their options. You can make recommendations, but you can't make them do anything. If you've built enough trust in your relationship, you can influence them (as you learned in Chapter 3), but you can't force their hand.

Most agents don't understand this, so they make themselves crazy and end up taking the blame for everything that doesn't go their way. Stop it. It's worse than unnecessary. It's burning you out, wrecking your client relationships, and getting in the way of actually solving problems. I can't tell you how many times I've listened to agents torturing themselves and beating themselves up for things that were never in their control. It's a very bad habit that agents need to address if they're going to have any level of sanity in their lives.

In this chapter, you'll learn to own your role as the trusted advisor. Once again, it comes down to detaching yourself from the outcome—leaving your feelings, desires, and need for control behind so your client can make the decisions that are rightfully theirs. It will take a huge weight off your shoulders, moving you one step closer to feeling truly joyful and at peace in your work.

## THE OLD WAY: TRY TO SOLVE EVERYTHING

If you're like most agents, you never made a conscious decision to try to solve every problem and make every decision in the sales process.

You just have this gut feeling that you *need* to. When a problem or choice comes up, your instinct is to tackle it, and you never think twice about whether it's yours to tackle.

It feels like an instinct because it comes from a very old emotion: fear. You're afraid of what the outcome of the process will be if you don't dictate every move.

Agents get so attached to the outcome in part because they sell their services on the basis of promises about that outcome. When you overpromise to win a client, then you feel responsible for fulfilling the promise. At a conscious level, you're afraid that if you don't, they'll walk away, or if they stick it out, they'll be unhappy with the result and bad-mouth you. Unconsciously, your brain is taking that train of thought to its "logical" conclusion: if you lose your clients, your business will fail, you'll go broke, end up on the streets, and *die*.

Thus, the fear...but none of that is real.

We've been through this before—you won't die. On the contrary, if you stop grasping for control and detach yourself from the outcome, you'll actually get out of your own way, just as you did in Chapter 3.

Think of all the things you take responsibility for that you have no real control over. If you're like the agents we coach, the list is long: pricing, staging, when to list, when to hold open houses, choosing a buyer, making offers and counteroffers, accepting or rejecting offers, handling inspection issues...and all the other miscellaneous problems that pop up in every deal.

You don't have the final say in any of this, but you try to convince, or even make decisions for, your clients anyway. After all, they hired you for your expertise, so you know what's best. They'll appreciate you taking the lead as the expert, right?

Not so much. In fact, not at all. Not even a little bit.

Never forget: people will die over their autonomy (see Chapter 1). When you take decisions away from them, or push them to choose, they resent you for it. You know this—just think about the last time you felt pressured to make a choice. Did you like that? Of course not. Neither do your clients, or anyone else.

Plus, taking responsibility for everything makes your life miserable. Anxiety and guilt pile up when things don't go perfectly, which is usually. You blame yourself, and the client does too, because when you took on responsibility, they gave it up. Everyone ends up in a negative emotional state, and the relationship starts to unravel.

## THE NEW WAY:
## ADVISE AND GUIDE

Let's go back one more time to how you and your clients start out on opposite sides of the street. Instead of yelling at them to come over to your side, first you need to cross to their side and stand shoulder to shoulder with them. Then, you have to look at the view from their perspective and see where they wanted to go.

Now comes the next step: gently guiding them to their destination.

Taking responsibility that isn't yours is like grabbing them by the wrist and dragging them up the road. Even if you're taking them where they want to go, they don't want to go like that.

Instead, just point out the possible paths, let them choose, and walk by their side to be there when they need more guidance. That's the only way to preserve their autonomy, which is a crucial element in building trust, cultivating influence, and making the experience positive for them regardless of where they end up. If they feel in control, they're more likely to feel satisfied with the final outcome, and even if they don't, they won't blame you.

You are not responsible for the outcome—you are accountable for doing what you say you are going to do. Your job is to lay out the landscape as best as possible. The client has to choose what direction they want to go.

---

### Two-millimeter Shift:
### Responsibility ➔ Accountability

You are not responsible for the outcome—you are accountable for doing what you say you are going to do. Your only job is to give your client the information they need to make their own decisions with confidence.

---

Remember, the only things you really have control over are how you market the listing (on the sell side) or how you search for listings (on the buy side), and how you conduct yourself with other agents. Everything else is beyond your power. It's all up to the client, and you can only educate and guide them.

## IT MATTERS WHO SAYS IT

Let's say you have a client who insisted on an inflated asking price and, as a result, hasn't received any offers. I bet this has happened to you before, so if you can recall a specific instance with a real client, think about that situation for a moment. Remember how you felt and how they felt after months of crickets from the market.

Now, imagine this: you say to your client, "We need to cut the price by 10 percent."

How do you feel as you're saying it? Probably some combination of anxious, frustrated, apologetic, and exhausted. You *need* them to agree, or the listing will expire without selling, and all this work will have been for nothing.

How does the client feel? Not too jazzed either, I'm sure. You said before that the house could sell at this price, and they had their heart set on it. Now, all they see is a 10 percent loss, and it was your idea, so it's on you.

Okay, now back up. What if, instead, *your client* said to *you*, "We need to cut the price by 10 percent."

That's a totally different ballgame. Instead of being at loggerheads, suddenly you're collaborating. They might not be thrilled to cut the price, but they're doing it willingly to get what they really want: a sold house. They understand that trade-off and have chosen to make it of their own free well, without pressure or coercion. You, needless to say, are massively relieved and happy to help them execute the decision they've made.

It's the same idea as the first scenario, even the exact same words, but it came out of your client's mouth instead of yours. That's what we mean when we say it matters who says it.

When it comes to guiding and influencing your clients, think about it this way: whatever you want them to do, they need to think it's their idea. At the very least, they need to feel it was 100 percent their choice to pursue that idea.

---

### Two-millimeter Shift:
### Leading ➜ Guiding

Taking the lead in the decision making process violates your client's autonomy. Instead, provide the information they need to navigate the decision while letting them stay in the driver's seat.

---

How would Victoria get Jasmine to say they need to cut the price by 10 percent? By playing the role of the trusted advisor. Remember, advisors don't make decisions, and they don't tell their clients what they need to do. They don't *need* to do anything, and you can't make them. All the advisor does is lay out the options and the likely consequences of each one.

So, she might say something like this, in her most deferential and respectful tone of voice: "With the house priced at $5 million, we haven't received any offers in over two months. If you keep that asking price, the house could remain unsold for six months or more. If you reduce the price to $4.5 million, we're likely to find a buyer within a couple of weeks, possibly multiple buyers. How would you like to proceed?"

First, she stated the facts of the situation. Then, she laid out the alternatives, stating them clearly as the *client's* choices. Obviously, Victoria favors one option over the other, but instead of saying so, she just emphasized the loss the client would experience if she didn't choose that option: the house would *remain unsold.* (That's bending reality, from Chapter 3.)

Finally, she put the ball squarely in Jasmine's court by asking her to own the choice. Not pressuring her to choose or suggesting which choice would be best—just giving her the space to consider the options, with her autonomy fully intact.

## NOTHING IS PERSONAL

One of the greatest dangers of taking on responsibilities that aren't yours is that you'll feel that you can't bring up a problem until you have a solution. Agents feel that if they're delivering bad news, they have to fix it—they can't just let the client sit with it and make the decisions about how to deal with it. So, they don't get the elephants out early like they should.

When you do this, your mind isn't on the client's needs—it's on you. More specifically, it's on your fear of how the client will respond to you. Because you don't want the client mad at you, you don't share what the client needs to know to make an intelligent decision. You put them at a disadvantage to protect your own ego.

But it's not about you. *Nothing in this business is ever about you.*

I said it in Chapter 3, and again in Chapter 4, and I'll say it one more time now: your emotions and desires have no place here. (Spoiler alert: I'll probably say it again before the book is done.)

How you feel is irrelevant, but for so many agents, that dictates how they behave. Plus, when your vision is clouded by your emotions, you can't read your clients, and you certainly can't make them feel understood. How can they feel understood when all your attention is on you?

When an issue comes up and you start to have feelings about it— whether that's anxiety, frustration, anger, hope, or anything else—the first step is to recognize that you're having thoughts and emotions about this. Label them, just like you do when you're preparing an Accusations Audit. Then, acknowledge what's driving them: your fear of what will happen if you don't control the process.

Remind yourself that you are not in control. You cannot decide, only advise. You're not here to steer the process, only to find out where it will go. When you detach from the outcome, you can finally become the trusted advisor your client wants and needs.

Your feelings hold you back from that, so just let them go. Breathe, meditate, calm yourself down in whatever way works for you. I promise it gets easier with practice.

## EMPATHY, NOT SYMPATHY

Like any new, learned behavior, it's normal to struggle with it or feel some resistance. One common source of resistance is the cultural idea that you help someone else by feeling their pain. Emotions are contagious—that's just human nature. When we see people smiling, we smile. When we see people get upset, we get upset. Just put a few babies together and wait: when one of them cries, the others start crying too.

But there's a reason we call it Tactical Empathy and not tactical sympathy. Are the other crying babies helping the first baby by sharing its emotional experience? Nope. That's sympathy, and it's natural, but not very useful in this situation. You feeling upset on your client's behalf is equally ineffective.

Tactical Empathy is the art of articulating what someone else is thinking and feeling, *without* necessarily agreeing or feeling the same way. That not only makes them feel understood, but it also prevents a disastrous feedback cycle of negative emotions between the two of you. Not only do you not need to feel bad about their problem (and remember, it is *their* problem), but you can be much more helpful if you don't.

If you stay calm and detached from the outcome, you can just lay out the facts and the options, then let them sit with the information until they're ready to make a decision.

I'll end this chapter with a real life example of an agent who had to put the responsibility where it belonged in a big way to move forward with a client. The agent had been working with the seller for four months already, preparing the house for sale. The price was originally going to be $3.95 million, which made sense for the market at that time. The agent wanted the seller to do $30,000 of work to get the house market ready, and the seller was reluctant but agreed.

Then, three weeks before going on the market, the agent spoke to a trusted colleague who worked in the area, and his fellow agent thought the price was closer to $3.5 million. All of a sudden, panic took over. *What if the price really is $3.5 million? What if I just had my seller spend $30,000 on staging that they wouldn't have spent if they knew the price was only $3.5 million? How am I going to explain this? What are they going to think of me? What if I don't tell them? What if I just wait to see how the market responds to the higher price?*

The agent did *not* want to have this conversation with the seller. He worried and berated himself for days, imagining what the client would say and trying to find a solution before he had to break the news. The emotional agony made those days miserable, even when he wasn't actively working at all.

But look at what he was taking responsibility for: the movements of the market and the seller's asking price. He didn't control either of those things, and he couldn't solve this problem. He could only educate the seller about the new reality, and allow him to decide how to proceed.

The agent didn't need a solution, and he didn't need all that angst either. All he needed was to detach from the outcome, put the responsibility where it belonged, and get the elephants out early (complete with an Accusations Audit).

In the end, the agent figured out that $3.95 million was actually the right price. The property was listed at that price and sold quickly at full asking. All of this back and forth and mental anguish was totally unnecessary. Even if the price had needed to be lowered to $3.5 million, it was always going to be the seller's decision. What the client needed was simply a clear picture of the options, and the autonomy to make the choice that was best for him. Would he have been happy if he had to lower the price by $500,000? Of course not. But instead of feeling blindsided by the situation and manipulated into a decision, he would have appreciated the agent's transparency and professionalism. That's the power of being a trusted advisor.

# KEY TAKEAWAYS

→ Agents habitually take responsibility for problems and decisions that aren't theirs, which causes huge amounts of unnecessary stress and work.

→ You don't own any of the decisions in this process. Only your client can make them, and when you try to do that for them, it violates their autonomy.

→ You can only advise and guide them. Your only job is to provide the information they need to make a decision with confidence.

→ When they decide for themselves—even if you guide them— they will be more committed to their choice and collaborative in implementing it with your help.

→ It's not helpful for you to get upset about problems on their behalf. You can understand their feelings without sharing them, and you're better equipped to guide them from a place of calm than a place of stress.

Chapter 6

# LET THEM SAY NO

*People hate to say yes, but*
*they love to say no.*

You've probably heard of momentum selling. It's that decades-old strategy where the salesperson asks a prospect a series of questions, all of which are designed to elicit a yes answer. Even if you've never heard the phrase "momentum selling," you've definitely had it done to you by a telemarketer or sidewalk fundraiser.

For example, here's a classic listing presentation technique taught by a leading real estate trainer:

Agent: Do you absolutely have to sell your home?
Prospect: Yes.
Agent: Do you want to get top dollar?
Prospect: Yes.
Agent: Do you want me to handle the sale?

119

Prospect: Yes.

Allegedly, it's that simple.

From the salesperson's perspective, momentum selling is an attractive idea. All you have to do is ask the right series of questions, and people will feel like they *have* to say yes to your offer. It makes sense on the surface: people don't like to contradict themselves, especially not in an obvious, public way, right? So, if you get them to say yes to easy, non-committal questions, they'll be more likely to say yes to an offer that's aligned with those answers.

The rule of thumb is that if a person says yes three times, you've succeeded—you'll get a sale. Each yes is a tie down, and by the time you've got three, most people won't be able to escape.

If you're wondering whether that's as sleazy and manipulative as it sounds, the answer is yes.

Buyers *hate* this tactic. Why do you think people hang up on telemarketers and avoid eye contact with sidewalk fundraisers? They know what's coming, and they don't want to get trapped. When they do get caught in a momentum selling ambush, they might say yes, but their actions probably won't support their words.

So, why do so many salespeople (including real estate agents) still do it? Well, it *seems* to work. At least, it can bring your closing rate to something more like 5–10 percent. For someone whose closing rate was close to zero, that could be a tenfold increase! You can't argue with that, can you?

Well, we're gonna.

If you've been paying attention, you knew that already. This way of selling goes against everything you've learned so far. If you're only pursuing opportunities where you're the Favorite, your closing rate should be closer to 100 percent than 10, and you don't need underhanded tactics to achieve that because those prospects chose you before you ever met them. And if you're building a business on trust instead of value, undermining your clients' autonomy by trapping them into saying yes is a surefire way to fail.

Salespeople are obsessed with yes. Even if they're not using momentum selling in this stereotypically slimy way, they're looking for other ways to get to that magic word. Every yes is a victory.

Not for clients, though. What feels like a win to you feels like vulnerability to them. When they say yes, it's usually with caution, wariness, and skepticism. That emotional state is not at all conducive to building a trusting relationship where they enjoy working with you and are open to your influence. You want your clients to feel safe and in control, not vulnerable and guarded.

So instead of *yes*, you're going to aim for *no*.

That probably sounds crazy. In business, yes means progress, and no means getting stalled. How can it possibly be productive to aim for no?

In this chapter, you'll find out.

## THE OLD WAY: PUSH FOR YES

For a moment, think like a regular person, not a salesperson. When someone approaches you with an offer or request, what's your first instinct? If you had to give a yes or no response within half a second, before you've had time to think about it, what would you say?

No. Every single time, no.

When you walk into a store and the salesperson immediately asks if they can help you find anything, you say no, even if you *are* looking for something specific.

When a stranger calls and asks if it's a good time to talk, you say no, even if you're not busy.

When your teenage kid asks to borrow the car, you say no, even if there's no good reason.

No is safe. It's the status quo. When you're not sure if something will be good for you, you protect yourself by pushing it away. Even when you do end up saying yes after you consider the situation, your very first instinct was to say no.

That's why salespeople try to use questions that couldn't possibly have any answer other than yes. *Do you want to make more money? Do you care about children? Could you spare a dime a day?* If you say no, you feel like a liar, an idiot, or a jerk.

It can be more subtle too. Back in the day (before I met Chris), I wrote tons of sales scripts designed to lead people down a very reasonable, logical path to yes. *Do you want to net the most money possible? Do you want a strong negotiator representing you? Do you want to make sure you're not leaving any money on the table?*

Like I said before, that stuff works. At least, it works better than *not* doing it...if you're trying to sell your value to every person that walks in your door.

Those sales scripts do get people to agree, and salespeople celebrate every yes they get, but they shouldn't. Those victories are hollow, and liable to disappear at any moment.

Think about it—when you get pressured into saying yes to a question that couldn't possibly have any other answer, you're suspicious. What does this person want from you, and how are you going to keep them from manipulating you? So you say yes, but it's not real. You're just leading them on to find out what else they're going to say...and how you can get out of this conversation gracefully.

That's what you're doing to your clients when you use momentum selling. They'll say yes to make you happy and get you off their back, but they probably don't mean it. In the meantime, you've undermined their trust in you by threatening their autonomy. Next time you talk, they'll approach the conversation with resistance ready to go in advance.

We don't want rejection, so why do we keep doing things that invite it?

It's like a slot machine. Most of the time, you strike out. But every once in a while, you win one, and it feels so good that you forget all the losses. So, you keep pulling, even though that thing is going to bankrupt you eventually.

It's time to kick the yes habit.

## THE NEW WAY: MASTER NO

People hate to say yes, but they love to say no. Once they've said no, they're actually more open to listening to you because they've protected themselves and established their control over the situation. Their autonomy is intact, and you aren't threatening it, so they actually have the mental space to process what you're saying.

So, start by triggering a no on purpose. Instead of asking questions designed to lead to yes, ask questions where a no serves you, a.k.a. a **no-oriented question**. For example:

- *Would you be opposed* to me sharing a story?
- *Would it be unreasonable* to do a Zoom call before I visit the property?
- *Would it be impossible* to stage the property before we list it?
- *Are you totally against* the idea of us working together?
- *Would it be wrong* to assume you've formed an impression of whether you want to work with me?
- *Would it be crazy* to think you have a price in mind?
- *Would it be out of line* to ask if you're considering other agents?
- *Would it be off base* to say you're looking to sell quickly?

You can take the beginnings of those sentences and finish them with whatever you want—whatever would make a no work in your favor. You're not restricted to that formula, though. Any yes-oriented question can be turned around into a no-oriented question or statement.

LET THEM SAY NO

**Tool: No-Oriented Question**

A question designed to elicit a no response, where no moves the conversation forward instead of shutting it down.

For example, shop salespeople usually ask, "Can I help you find anything?" If they really want to help you (maybe they work on commission), they should say, "You probably know what you're looking for and don't need my help."

Here's a common one: when you call people, you probably ask, "Is now a good time to talk?" Instead, you should ask, "Is now a bad time to talk?"

They could say, "Yes, it's a bad time, I'm very busy," but they usually don't. Why? *Because people love to say no.* It's not a logical thing—it's emotional. No matter which question you ask, the first thing they want to say is no. So, ask the question where no moves the conversation forward.

You'll see this for yourself when you try it with your prospects. You know sellers expect agents to come give a listing presentation, and you also now know that this free consulting is killing your business. It's not necessary, or a good use of your time, and you want to avoid doing it.

Here's how you use a no-oriented question to achieve that: *Would you be opposed to doing a video call before I come out to the house?*

They almost always say no.

Turn it into a yes-oriented question (*Could we do a video call before I come out to the house?*), and you'll get a very different response: resistance. *Why do we need to do that? Why is this person asking something unexpected of me?* They want to say no, and with this yes-oriented question, no is unhelpful.

No-oriented questions unlock all kinds of barriers. When people feel safe, they'll listen more openly, offer information more freely, and collaborate more readily.

## CALIBRATED QUESTIONS™ [12]

The key to all that information and collaboration is calibrated questions. These are open-ended questions that are calibrated to put the other person in an open frame of mind towards you. Usually, they're how or what questions. For example:

- What would need to happen...?
- What would that look like?
- What criteria are most important to you?
- What should the next step be?
- How should we proceed?
- How will you decide?
- How would you see us working together?

---

[12] One of the Black Swan Method Negotiation 9 Skills. More in-depth training on the Negotiation 9 is available at www.blackswanltd.com.

LET THEM SAY NO

With these questions, you're showing deference to the other person, which warms them to you. People love to be asked what they think. It makes them feel respected, valued, and heard.

---

### Tool: Calibrated Questions

Open-ended questions (almost always beginning with how or what) designed to put the other person in an open frame of mind towards you.

---

You're also prompting them to think deeply. This stops people in their tracks, and forces them to carefully consider whatever situation or choice you've put in front of them. Instead of dwelling on their emotional reaction to it, they focus on solving the problem or clarifying their desires and intentions, within the safety of their own autonomy.

That's why these questions are so effective at revealing important information and inviting collaboration with your clients. As you learned in Chapter 5: whatever you want them to do, they need to think it's their idea.

Before you can break out the how and what questions, first make them feel understood. Use mirrors and labels to get them to say "that's right" (flip back to Chapter 2 for a refresher on this). You'll feel that emotional click when you get in alignment with them, and that's when you can start guiding them to where they want to go.

How and what questions put the ball in the other person's court and make them think. Their answers reveal what they will and won't do, so you don't have to guess. Here are some examples of calibrated questions that can work in many situations throughout the real estate sales process:

- What are you really hoping for?
- What is important to you about that?
- What would make this a great experience for you?
- What is most important to you during this process?
- What are your biggest concerns?
- What are you basing that on?
- What have I left out?
- What else do we need to discuss?
- What happens if...?
- What would need to happen...?
- How would you like me to do that?
- How long do you want to try that?
- How will you know...?
- How do you see that happening?
- How do you want to handle this?
- How are you going to decide?
- How do you see this playing out?
- How are you going to feel if...?
- How have you done this in the past?
- How do you like to...?

## DON'T TAKE THE BAIT

This chapter has been all about asking questions. That's how you focus on the other person—it's standing shoulder to shoulder and seeing what they're seeing. It's a huge part of the trust-building process.

But, as you already know, salespeople like to answer questions, not ask them. You've been trained that your value is in having all the answers. You think: *If I don't have the answer, why would anyone work with me?*

So, you jump to answer questions because it's a chance to demonstrate your value...especially when they ask, "What do you think?" That's your favorite one.

Don't take the bait!

Your clients don't want to know what you think. They only want to know if you think what they think. They already have something in mind, but they're just not ready to commit to it quite yet.

The real question is, *why* do they want to know what you think? This is the moment to find out. What's the thought that's already in their mind, and what are their feelings around it? If they're not confident in their decision yet, where is that uncertainty coming from? What are they afraid of, and what other information do they need to move forward?

Labels and calibrated questions will help you find out. Tailor them to the situation—start with a phrase like "It seems like you have doubts about..." or "What would you need to know to decide..." and fill in the specifics. Keep going until you have a clear understanding of why they're stuck.

That's how you help them get unstuck—not by simply making a recommendation but by digging down to the root of the issue and solving it at that level.

In the end, it's always on you to put the ball back in their court: "If it were me, this is what I would do...But it's not me, it's you, and it's your decision to make. How do you want to proceed?"

# KEY TAKEAWAYS

→ As a salesperson, you're trained to get to yes, and it feels great when you do. But for the customer, saying yes makes them feel vulnerable and wary.

→ What people really want to say is no because it feels safe. No preserves the status quo and protects their autonomy.

→ So, begin with no-oriented questions. Once they've said no, they'll be more open to your guidance.

→ Then, use calibrated questions to prompt them to think deeply and share their thoughts with you.

→ If they ask what you think, don't take the question at face value. Dig deeper to uncover what they're already thinking, and why they feel uncertain about it.

## Tactical Empathy Toolbox

→ **No-Oriented Questions:** Questions designed to elicit a no response, where no moves the conversation forward instead of shutting it down.

→ **Calibrated Questions:** Open-ended questions (usually beginning with how or what) designed to put the other person in an open frame of mind towards you.

## Chapter 7

# NAIL THE LASTING IMPRESSION

*Send people away in a limo, and there's
a good chance they'll come back.*

IMAGINE YOU'RE REPRESENTING A SELLER AT THE END OF A DEAL.
You've got an offer from a serious buyer, you got the inspection done, and
you've spent a week going back and forth, trying to get both parties to a
place where they can agree. You've resolved every negotiation point and
are only $3,000 apart on price.

So, you do what most agents would do: you split the difference. The
seller and the buyer each eat $1,500. It's a simple, fair solution, right? Your
client doesn't love it, but you convince them it's the only surefire way to
close the deal. They agree to it because you've invested weeks into this
process now, and the last thing they want is to relist and start again from
scratch.

Finally, the deal is done. It only took two months from the time the seller contacted you. They wanted to sell quickly, so you see that as a huge win. Plus, they got almost their full asking price and only had to make a few repairs. You think they should be thrilled— thrilled enough to work with you again in the future, or send referrals your way.

But they're not. They don't say anything negative to your face, but they just don't seem as ecstatic as you thought they'd be. You never hear from them again, and they never send anyone your way. What happened?

You didn't think about the last impression. Everyone tells you to worry about first impressions because you only get one chance. Sure, but usually there's at least a little time to recover if it doesn't go well.

Not so with the last impression. That's the feeling that sticks, and because it's last, you really don't get another chance. And for a business built on repeat and referral customers—as yours should be—you can't afford to neglect the last impression.

In this story, everything went smoothly until the end of the deal. But what stuck in the client's mind was that last concession, the one they were reluctant to make, but felt like they had to. It wasn't even a lot of money in the grand scheme of things, but it felt bad, like the buyer got something they shouldn't have, and you couldn't prevent it. The seller got almost everything they wanted, but that sour taste from the end of the negotiation is what they'll remember.

This happens *all the time,* and most of the time you don't even know it. In this industry, 90 percent of buyers and sellers say they would work with the same agent again, but only 20 percent ever actually do. Yikes.

At the very beginning of this book, I showed you why repeat and referral business has to be the foundation of your work. It's the only way to run a successful real estate business that allows you to actually enjoy your life. It's a natural consequence of doing business as a human being instead of a commodity.

In this chapter, you'll learn how to make sure your lasting impression is the kind that will bring people back for more.

## THE OLD WAY:
## EVERY CLOSED DEAL IS A WIN

Agents love closing deals. It's what puts money in their pocket and sends their production numbers up. It's what they brag about. It's what they live for.

For an agent, every closed deal brings a massive sigh of relief. There's always the chance that all your hard work could come to nothing at the last minute. When it doesn't, that's cause for celebration. You assume that your clients feel the same way.

They might...but they might not. It's not about how close the deal ended up being to what they originally wanted. That would be logical, but as you already know, there's way more going on in the human mind than just logic.

It's about the quality of the emotional experience they had in getting to the deal, especially at the end. Did they feel like they were fully informed and in control of their decisions, or like they were roped into things they weren't really okay with? Did they feel like they made the

THE FULL FEE AGENT

right trade-offs to get what really mattered to them, or like they gave up more than they should have? Do they feel you protected their interests and helped them make the right decisions, or you just wanted to get the deal done?

That's what really matters.

So no, every closed deal is not a win. It's only a win if the client *feels* like they won. It doesn't matter what the deal looks like on paper—only their emotional experience of it. Your goal isn't to close the deal. It's to make sure they walk away happy, regardless of the business outcome.

## THE NEW WAY:
## FOLLOW THE OPRAH RULE

The last impression is the lasting impression—Chris knew this intuitively from his hostage negotiation work, but he first heard it articulated and verified at a Gallup conference in 2008. You know Gallup, the company that does all those polls you hear about in the news. They had a mountain of data about human behavior and how people recall past events, and the evidence was right there.

People don't remember how it happened. They remember the most intense moment and how it ended.

That explained why Chris and his FBI teammates had been able to get the upper hand in multiple hostage situations just by taking control of the *end* of each conversation with the kidnappers. If the kidnapper had a habit of hanging up with no warning or putting the call on hold, the FBI team focused on getting him to finish the conversation properly: say goodbye and hang up. That's civilized and respectful behavior, and it completely changed the emotions and balance of power in the negotiation.

After the conference, Chris talked about the idea of the lasting impression with his friend Cindy Mori, who was Oprah's booker at the time. "Of course," she said. In most of the entertainment industry, you come in a limo and leave in a taxi. Not with Oprah. On her show, you come in a limo and leave in a limo, literally and figuratively.

Of the thousands of people who went on that show over twenty-five years, who comes to mind who has bad-mouthed Oprah? There were never any serious public spats or feuds, and any rumors along those lines disappeared quickly because her guests only ever had nice things to say about their experiences. People loved how it felt to go on Oprah as much as they loved to watch it, which is why she was able to get so many famous and powerful people to come back again and again.

That's what you're aiming for. Send people away in a limo, and there's a good chance they'll come back.

This doesn't just apply to clients who close deals with you. It applies to *everyone*, no matter the circumstances under which they walk away from you. That includes prospects who decide not to work with you, and clients who decide to let their listings expire unsold or switch to another agent. It also includes other people who work with you, like the other party's agent or vendors for things like home staging and repairs.

When people walk away happy, they come back again later, ready to collaborate with you again...and that makes your life *so* much easier.

You already know that customer acquisition costs are what really kill real estate agents. All the time and money you spend finding clients eats away at your bottom line like a termite infestation. But when a customer comes back for more or sends you a referral, that business lands in your lap practically for free. You need as much of that as you can get.

Plus, it's much more productive and enjoyable to work with someone who already has a positive relationship with you, or at least a positive impression. Without that, they're likely to be skeptical and guarded, which means you have to build trust from the ground up. It's doable, as you've learned, but it takes time. Working within an existing trusting relationship is that much more efficient.

So, how are you going to make sure everyone walks away happy?

## NEVER SPLIT THE DIFFERENCE™

Chris called his first book *Never Split the Difference* for good reason: everyone does it all the time, and it's always a bad idea.

Real estate agents are the guiltiest of all. Splitting the difference is the default solution to every negotiation problem. We see it all the time—every single one of my coaching clients reacts with shock and confusion when they learn they need to stop doing it. Most of the time, they have no idea what else to do.

You probably think Chris and I are crazy. What could be more fair and reasonable than a fifty-fifty compromise?

But compromise is never equal.

Let's go back to the story from the beginning of the chapter. When the seller agreed to split the $3,000 difference with the buyer, what really happened in their head?

Well, you learned in Chapter 1 that the pain of a loss is twice as powerful as the pleasure of an equivalent gain. So, that $1,500 loss *felt* like $3,000, whereas the other side only gave up half that. In theory, for your client to feel like the split was fair, they would give up just $1,000 while the other party ate $2,000. Splitting the difference down the middle is *never* going to feel good for your client.

When agents can't split the difference—or don't want to ask their client for another concession—they usually have one backup plan: chip in and cover the cost themselves. Agents are notorious for reaching in their own pockets to make a deal come together. You believe something is better than nothing, so to avoid losing the whole commission, you just sacrifice a little chunk of it.

You think you're securing your business by chipping in, but in reality, you're undermining it.

This is a sign that your business is based on explaining value, not building trust. Without trust, the only value you can offer that means anything to them is your time and money. So, to get as much out of you as possible, they treat you like a bank. Whenever they need your time or money to move the deal forward, they feel entitled to it. After all, that's effectively what you promised.

You think you're getting emotional bonus points for your generosity, but you're not. You're just setting the expectation that it's okay for your clients to reach into your pocket. Plus, you're confirming to them that your time is an unlimited free commodity and your money is cheap. What they perceive is that you can't even make a deal come together without opening your own wallet.

In a trust-based business, the client doesn't ask you to chip in. If you've built a strong relationship as their trusted advisor and consistently put the responsibility where it belongs, why would they? They understand that you're here to educate, support, and protect them—not to pay their bills. They're not looking for a discount because they know you're worth every penny, and they wouldn't want to disrespect you by implying that you don't deserve your fee.

When the transaction is the only thing that matters, you'll give things away to get it done. When the relationship is what matters most, you recognize that it's not healthy for one party to feel entitled to stick their hand in the other's pocket.

So, if you want your clients to feel like they're riding away in a limo, you can't split the difference, and you can't just chip in to make the problem go away. You've got to do something different.

I don't mean some kind of special negotiation tactic or closing trick. In fact, you've already learned exactly what to do.

## MAKE THEM FEEL UNDERSTOOD

That's it: practice Tactical Empathy. Make them feel understood.

You did this at the beginning of the relationship, when you were finding out if you were the Favorite or the Fool. You did it when you were building trust, breaking bad news, and guiding them to make informed decisions. You need to keep doing it until the very end—*especially* at the very end.

The end of a deal process is a test of your commitment to Tactical Empathy. As you get closer and closer, you'll be more and more tempted to default to your old salesperson habits. You'll get impatient and start looking for the first opportunity to close, pushing everyone else, including your client, to get there faster. The fear will creep in, and bait you into throwing Tactical Empathy to the wind. This is why you often feel like no good deed goes unpunished.

Don't give up.

Go back to what you've learned in this book. When you detach yourself from the outcome, you get out of your own way. Just give your best effort as an authentic human being who is here to serve others, and the results will take care of themselves.

How you behave at this stage should be no different from what you've done up to this point. First, you prepare for every conversation by thinking through (and ideally writing down) what everyone else is likely to be thinking and feeling.

For example, here are some things a potential seller might be thinking, in no specific order:

- Should I sell?
- What is my house worth?
- Will I get the price I want?
- Is now the right time to move?
- Does it make sense for me to sell my house in the current market?

THE FULL FEE AGENT

- How much money will I net?
- What are closing costs?
- What other costs are associated with selling?
- What does the selling process look like?
- How much time will it take to sell my house?
- How involved do I have to be in this process?
- Will the process be stressful?
- What agents should I interview?
- Do I really need an agent?
- Can I sell the house myself?
- What is a standard commission for an agent?
- Will I have to hold open houses?
- What will my neighbors think?
- Am I making the right decision?
- Where will I move to?
- Where do I begin?
- How do I feel about this?
- Will this be difficult?
- How do I go about finding the right agent?
- Why are different agents giving me conflicting information?
- Why are agents telling me a different number than Zillow?
- Should I put money into updating my home?
- Can I sell my home as is?
- What will buyers think of my home?
- Are buyers going to ask for credits or repairs?
- Will I be sad to leave this home?

- How much work do I have to do?
- What if the house doesn't sell?

Examine what you're thinking and feeling as well, and recognize that your thoughts and feelings have no place here and won't help you. Let them go.

Then, during the conversation, you listen with your full attention to the other person. Use mirroring, labeling, and mislabeling to elicit more information and make them feel heard. Aim to get to "that's right." When you feel that click of emotional alignment, you'll know they feel understood.

That's when you can start guiding them to where they want to go. Lay out the landscape for them: the facts of the present situation, the options they have, and the likely consequences of each option. Then, use calibrated questions to make them think about (and reveal to you) what they truly want and don't want. Only they can decide what to do, so give them the space to do that with a simple question: *How would you like to proceed?*

Don't fall into the trap of thinking your role as the expert is to tell them what to do. Even if they act like that's what they want, it's not. They're just scared—this is a big decision, probably the biggest financial transaction of their life, and they don't want to screw it up.

That doesn't mean they actually want you to decide for them. They just want to feel empowered to make a decision with confidence.

The key to that isn't giving your opinion or recommendation. It's showing them the full decision landscape, and being transparent about the inherent uncertainties involved. Even you, the expert, can't say 100 percent for sure what the consequences of any given decision will be. You can share your best educated guess, and be honest about your level of certainty around it.

Give them all the information you would consider if you were making the decision for yourself...but don't make it. That's their job. When you do that, they will feel supported and in charge of their own destiny.

At no point in time do you try to convince them of anything. Be patient. You're not here to *make* something happen with fact, logic, and reason. You're here to explore the unknown and *find out* what will happen.

## LIMOS FOR EVERYONE

That's what makes people walk away with a positive emotional experience of interacting with you. It even works when they decide *not* to work with you.

For example, let's say you're talking to a prospect, and they've got their heart set on an inflated asking price. You strongly believe the house won't sell at that price point, and you know it would be a waste of time and bad for the client relationship to accept the listing at that price, only to have to reduce it later.

So, you use the same process. First, you listen with your full attention and make them feel understood. Then you lay out the situation: your view is that the market won't support that asking price, and you wouldn't want to waste the seller's time pretending that it does.

It seems like you are committed to listing your home at $X or above. You've probably spoken to an agent who feels confident they can get you that price. Unfortunately, I see the market differently. You deserve to work with someone who believes in your price.

If the seller wants to go with someone else, that's okay! It's their prerogative. Send them away in a limo anyway with this offer: *If for any reason things don't work out, and you feel I can help you, please feel free to reach out and contact me.*

You made them feel understood, allowed them to make an empowered decision, and ended on a positive note. When their listing expires with that other agent, they'll be back.

# KEY TAKEAWAYS

→ The last impression is the lasting impression. If a deal closes in a way that doesn't feel good to the client, that negative emotion is what they'll remember.

→ That's a huge problem for your business. People who walk away unhappy won't work with you again, or refer others to you.

→ Follow the Oprah Rule: send everyone away in a limo. That means practicing Tactical Empathy in every relationship, all the way to the end.

→ Splitting the difference and chipping in to make a deal come together are lazy tactics that undermine your relationship with the client. Don't give into the temptation to use them—practice Tactical Empathy instead.

→ All of this applies to every relationship, regardless of whether the person chooses to do business with you now. If you send them away in a limo, they're more likely to come back again.

## Chapter 8

# BE A FULL-SERVICE, FULL FEE AGENT

*At 6 percent, real estate agents are the biggest bargain on the planet.*

WHEN YOU GET THE LISTING INTERVIEW PHONE CALL, IN YOUR HEAD, you are a 6 percent agent.

In your car going to the appointment, your fee is now 5.5 percent, with you keeping 3 percent.

As you get out of your car to go to the front door, your fee is now 5 percent.

When they answer the door, you blurt out unprovoked, "My fee is 4.5 percent!"

Does this sound familiar in any way?

If you want to know what it means to be a full-service, full fee agent, look no further than Regina Vannicola.

THE FULL FEE AGENT

THE FULL FEE AGENT

THE FULL FEE AGENT

She's one of our coaching clients, and like every agent who works with us, she used to be in the habit of making herself into a doormat. She prided herself on doing whatever it took to get the listing and close the sale, and if that meant discounting her fee or caving to crazy client demands, she did it.

Virtually all agents do. It's not that they like being doormats—no one does. They're just afraid of what will happen if they don't.

After learning what you've learned in this book, Regina decided to be brave and find out. When a developer called her about listing a unit he was converting from an apartment into a condo, she went to see the property with a new mindset: Not, *What do I have to do to get this listing?* But, *Is this opportunity a good fit?*

This developer was a mover and shaker who owned lots of income properties in the community. Obviously, he was an old hand at real estate deals, and because so many agents discount their fees, Regina had doubts about whether he'd be willing to pay her full fee.

So, instead of avoiding the issue, she got the elephants out early. After touring the property, she said, "I've got some things we need to talk about that could be deal breakers for you. This is going really well, but I might throw a wrench in the works with this information, so I'd like to put it on the table now. Would you be opposed?

"No, go ahead," the developer said.

"Here's my top ten list of reasons why you won't want to work with me."

"*Ten?*" he asked.

"Well, no, there are really only about four," she said, and the developer laughed. She continued, "First and foremost, I'm a full-service, full fee agent. I charge 6 percent, keep 3.5 percent, and give 2.5 percent to the buyer's agent. I'm going to encourage you to price the property so that it will sell quickly, and that might very well be a price that's less than what you'd like to see. I'm going to encourage you to invest in preparing it for sale, and you're going to need to stage it. The last thing is that I don't work 24/7. You'll never need me and not get me, but you won't need me at 10 p.m., and my phone goes off at 6."

The developer took a step back and said, "Wow, that's a lot of conditions! We just met."

Regina laughed and said, "I actually prefer to think of them as standards."

He paused for a moment, then asked, "Why don't you split the commission equally with the buyer's agent?"

At that moment, she knew she was hired. He wasn't balking at her standards, just asking a question about a detail that wasn't an important factor in his decision. With that knowledge came an upwelling of self-worth, confidence, and power.[13]

Most agents cringe at the very thought of approaching a prospect with a list like that in the very first conversation (or any time, for that matter). But when Regina talks about doing it, she can't stop smiling.

Laying out the potential deal breakers—especially the commission —up front has saved her *massive* amounts of time and frustration. It quickly weeds out the bad clients, and the people who were never going

---

[13] Watch Regina tell this story in her own words: https://www.youtube.com/watch?v=22 DDQRIERlk.

to hire her anyway. What she's left with are clients who believe in her worth and are ready to work collaboratively.

Plus, she just doesn't have to sell as many homes to hit her income goals. Do the math: if you charge 5 percent and keep half, you have to sell *40 percent more homes* than if you charge 6 percent and keep 3.5 percent. How would your life be different if you had 40 percent more time for yourself, or 40 percent more income for the same amount of effort? A 1 percent difference might seem small, but don't be fooled—it will transform your business and life.

In this chapter, we'll tie together everything you've learned so far into the mother of all tough conversations: your standards...*especially* your commission.

You'll see that standing firmly by your fee isn't about being greedy. It's about being the best agent you can be for your clients. That might sound crazy now, especially if you're thinking there's no way you can get away with charging 6 percent in your market. By the end of this chapter, you'll see that it's not just sensible—it's imperative, for your sake and your clients'.

## THE OLD WAY: DOORMAT YOURSELF

Commission is the one topic that scares agents more than anything else. Everyone has an opinion, but no one wants to talk about it with an open mind. There's a select group of agents who charge a full fee on one side of the street, and then everyone else—a much bigger group—on the other side, with virtually no middle ground. There is an overwhelming belief that you cannot charge a full fee and thrive in this business. Everyone wants to pretend there is nothing they can do about it. *It's a losing battle,* they tell themselves. *What's the point in hashing it out again?*

And yet this is probably the most important conversation that needs to happen. Commission is where the rubber meets the road in real estate. Your ego, your value, your self-worth, your self-confidence, your pocketbook, your future—it's all up for grabs in that one moment when a potential seller asks, "What is your fee?"

That's all it takes to make a real estate agent squirm. I can get a discount from ninety-nine out of one hundred agents just by asking that one, simple question. The default response to even the slightest hint of pushback on your fee is to hand out a discount, even when the client hasn't actually asked for one.

Why?

It all comes back to fear. Fear that you're not really worth 6 percent after all. Fear of being an imposter. Fear of being rejected. Fear of what will happen if you lose this opportunity.

To that, we say *stop it!* Stop letting fear run your life, and stop giving your money away!

You work too hard and too long to just let people reach into your pocket as if they were entitled to do so. Every buyer and seller wants your money. Whether they ask up front or at the end of the transaction or somewhere in between, they're going to ask. Count on it. They always have a "legitimate" reason to ask, and you always have a "legitimate" reason to give in.

But the truth is, no one ever needs your money—they just want it because they think they can get it. If someone needs your $500 or

$1,000 or $10,000 or more to buy or sell a home, they shouldn't be doing the deal.

If only agents were as protective with their commission as they are with their split with their brokerage. How do you feel when your sales manager calls you into their office and says they need to lower your split? Do you just roll over? Of course not! But when a buyer or seller does the same thing, suddenly you become shy and small and timid. It makes no sense.

Bottom line: you *can* and *must* charge 6 percent.

As Chris always says, at 6 percent, real estate agents are the biggest bargain on the planet. In any other industry, a finder's fee is 10 percent.

I've coached enough agents that I know you can charge 6 percent in any market. It doesn't matter if your competitors are charging less. It doesn't matter if you're a super high-end agent working with multimillion-dollar listings. Save your excuses—we'll get to those in a minute. First, we need to fix a false assumption that's holding you back.

## THE NEW WAY: FULL SERVICE, FULL FEE

Imagine this for a moment: what if a prospect told you they didn't care about your fee? What if price just wasn't an important factor in deciding who to hire?

You would charge your full fee, of course. If you know without a doubt that they don't care, why wouldn't you?

Well, guess what? *They actually don't care.* I know this sounds insane, but just bear with me for a minute.

In one study of B2B sales, researchers broke down the sales process into nine steps, from the initial search for potential solutions all the way to engaging with a sales rep from the chosen vendor to make the purchase. Customers get pricing information in step three, but they don't reach out to vendors until step eight. In between, they're busy evaluating all their options and consulting with other people about the decision. By the time they talk to vendors, their mind is already 70–100 percent made up.

You already know this—it was one of the first things you learned in this book. When a prospect calls you, you're already the Favorite or the Fool.

Here's the crazy part. Customers know a vendor's price way back in step three. If they get all the way to step eight and contact that vendor, they've reconciled themselves to that price. Otherwise, they would have eliminated that option by then.

In fact, researchers asked what the most important factors were when evaluating vendors (step three) and making the final choice (step nine). At step three, price is the number one consideration. At step nine, it doesn't even make the top five. What they really care about is whether the solution is the right fit.

Whether it's B2B or B2C, humans are humans. If that's how they make major business purchases, it's how they make major personal purchases too, including hiring a real estate agent. They know long before they call you that 5 to 6 percent is the industry standard commission. By the time you talk to a prospect, price is *not* a major factor in their choice.

You already said it: if you knew a prospect didn't care about price, you would charge your full fee.

So from now on, that's what you're going to do.

## ARE YOU THE FAVORITE?

Here's the real secret to getting a full fee. It's not about providing more value, being more persuasive, or changing anyone's mind. (You know by now that none of that has any place in your business anymore.)

It's a function of one thing only: are you the Favorite or the Fool?

If you're the Favorite, they'll pay your full fee. They might ask questions or push back a little, but they'll pay it in the end.

If you're the Fool, it doesn't matter what your fee is—they're most likely not going to hire you. If you chase every low-probability deal and keep handing out discounts, sure, you might convert some of those prospects. But at what cost?

Discounting is a hard habit to break. If you do it once, you'll do it again, and it can become a crutch very easily. That has long-term ramifications for your business that most agents never consider.

Here's an exercise that will make you sick to your stomach: go back to your first day in real estate and add up all the money you've given up by discounting or chipping in. Go on, do it. The total number will shock you.

You may think you never would have gotten some of that business if you hadn't discounted. Maybe, but you have no idea how much *more* business you would have done without those discount clients getting in the way.

As you learned back in Chapter 2, having to convince someone to work with you is a bad sign for the relationship. Those are the worst clients—skeptical, untrusting, and demanding—and one bad client takes up the space of two good clients. In other words, one discount client takes up the space of two full fee clients. If you've been operating under the illusion that discounting is good for your business, it's time to face reality.

Let's go back to something else from the very beginning of the book: you can't overcome emotion with fact, logic, and reason.

This statement is at the heart of every commission discussion. Sellers don't want to feel foolish by paying more than necessary—*feel* being the operative word here. You've probably studied all kinds of commission dialogues that try to convince people with facts, logic, and reason that you're worth what you charge...but you can't overcome emotion with facts, logic, and reason. There's no convincing anyone to feel less foolish.

People will pay you 6 percent because they *feel* they absolutely want to work with you. In every interaction, you've demonstrated qualities—like trustworthiness, competency, and transparency—that give that person confidence in your abilities. They know you're going to do what you say, and put their interests first at all times. They don't want to go through this process without you.

All because you made them *feel understood.*

Those are the clients you want. With them, you're the Favorite. They will gladly pay your full fee, collaborate with you, be open to your influence, and appreciate your hard work.

To make room for them, you have to walk away from everyone else. Make 6 percent your standard, and stick to it fearlessly. You're not afraid to have the commission conversation, and you're not afraid to say "no thank you" to those who aren't willing to pay 6 percent.

It's that simple. I've studied this from every angle possible, and the ability to charge 6 percent is not a function of market conditions, geography, list price, experience, or production. It depends on just this: do you have walk away power?

If you're not willing to walk away from anyone who won't pay you your full fee, you won't be successful charging 6 percent. End of story. Six percent needs to be a standard.

And as Clayton Christensen, a former Harvard Business School professor, said: it's easier to do something 100 percent of the time than 98 percent of the time.

From now on, you charge everyone 6 percent, no matter the situation or circumstance. If a seller can't accept your fee, that's okay—you just walk away.

Seriously, no exceptions. Just imagine a handful of your best clients getting together by some chance. The conversation comes around to you and what you charge. How would that conversation go? Would you be getting irate phone calls because you were charging different amounts to different people? How would that affect their trust in you and willingness to refer business to you or hire you again in the future?

Making 6 percent your standard is better for your business in so many ways...and it's also good for your clients. Charging a full fee forces you to become a better agent because to charge more, you have to provide exceptional value. To provide more value, you have to examine every aspect in your business: your mindset, strategy, prospecting, follow up, marketing, showing, negotiating, problem solving, and everything in between. Does it all align with a 6 percent fee?

In *The Science Of Getting Rich* by Wallace D. Wattles, the author says: "Give every person more in use value than you take from them in cash value. Then you are adding to the life of the world with every business transaction."

Challenge yourself to live up to your 6 percent fee. The irony is, you'll end up doing more business and making more money by becoming more conscious about the work you do, and the value people derive from it. At first, insisting on 6 percent sounds greedy and selfish, but the reality is the exact opposite: it keeps you on your toes, and inspires you to do your very best work at every opportunity.

## NO MORE EXCUSES

I know all the reasons why you feel you must lower your fee. *All of them.*

No matter what your excuse (and it is an excuse), the underlying reason is fear. You think there is not enough business out there for you. If you don't discount, you'll lose to someone else who will, and something is better than nothing. Time after time, you convince yourself there is no other option other than to concede. It's just the cost of doing business.

It's all B.S. The pull in this industry to discount is so strong, and there is such a herd mentality when it comes to your fee. So, let's address the most common excuses directly.

### Excuse #1: Discounting has always worked for me.

You've gotten this far, right? Why fix what's not broken? You've been discounting practically since day one, and you're convinced that it's a key reason for your success so far.

Chris likes to compare this to teenage boys shaving. At some point, every boy hears that shaving makes your facial hair grow faster and thicker. This isn't actually true, but they don't know it. So, the second a hair appears, they whip out the razor and have at it. Sure enough, they start to see more and more facial hair.

But that hair growing had nothing to do with the shaving. It was going to grow anyway, razor or no razor.

You think discounting is the reason you've won business...but is it? How do you know? Even if your clients said they'd go with someone else unless you reduce your fee, how can you be sure they weren't bluffing?

You can't. You also can't know what other business you might have won if you had let those discount clients walk.

You've already heard all the ways discounting is hurting your business without you even realizing it. So yeah, it's broken, and yeah, you do need to fix it.

### Excuse #2: No one will go for that—all the other agents charge less.

Over and over, agents tell me: *Six percent can't be done. No one in this market is doing that.*

The second part might be true, but that doesn't make the first part true.

In Chris's early days as an FBI hostage negotiator, no one ever asked the kidnappers to put the hostage on the phone. It couldn't be done, they said. When asked, the kidnappers always refused. It made getting proof of life (evidence that the hostage was, in fact, alive and in custody) extremely difficult.

But what if they asked in a different way? "Can I speak to the hostage?" was a yes-oriented question, and it wasn't working...but maybe a calibrated question would change the game. So, they tried it: "How do we know the hostage is alive?"

It worked. All it took was a little tweak in their approach, and something that couldn't be done suddenly became an extremely effective standard protocol.

We hear this excuse from most agents, but top performers and luxury agents are the biggest offenders. They fool themselves into thinking it's all about market share. More signs means more sales.

I don't disagree that more signs means more sales, but I do disagree with giving your money away to get more signs. If you're losing market share over commission, there's something else at play that you don't want to address. It's just easier to lower your fee than to closely examine the value you provide.

Anyone can give their money away. There is no skill or special talent in lowering your fee from 6 percent to 5 percent or 4 percent or lower. It's just the fear driven, lazy way to do business. But as Chris said in *Never Split The Difference*, "You've got to embrace the hard stuff. That's where the great deals are. And that's what great negotiators do."

Luxury agents also rationalize that they can afford to reduce their fee when the list price is so high. But in what other industry do the top professionals work for *less?*

Flip that rationalization around: if anyone can afford to pay a full fee, it's the high-end client. Those sellers have the money and are used to paying top dollar for what they really want. And when the list price is high, the value of a truly skilled agent is amplified. A great negotiator could mean a difference of hundreds of thousands or millions of dollars in the final sale price. If it takes a full fee agent to get that result, of course they'll pay.

I'm not just making this up. Our coaching clients include plenty of top agents, and we've seen them get full fees even in the top echelons of this business, where everyone says it's impossible. We just had one agent get 6 percent on a $10 million dollar listing. Another sold a $50 million dollar house last year at *7 percent.* It's not impossible. It's just a question of whether you're the Favorite or the Fool, and whether you're fearless enough to stick to your standards.

### Excuse #3: There's a special reason for a discount in this case.

There are all kinds of reasons for giving a discount. The client is a friend or family member or a repeat client or a referral or my kid's teacher or my spouse's boss's brother-in-law.

Here's my favorite: *If I represent both sides of the deal, I'll charge 4 percent.*

Whose idea was this? Somehow, this has become a standard practice in the industry, but how does this make sense in any way? When you double end a deal, you still have two jobs to do, and two sets of clients. Where is the logic in reducing your fee by 33 percent?

This same agent, who listed the $50 million dollar property at 7 percent, recently double-ended an $8.6 million dollar deal at 6 percent. During the negotiation, the seller asked the agent to reduce his fee to 4 percent. He simply said, with total deference and respect, "No. We can keep marketing the home to find a buyer who will pay more." The seller happily signed the deal. They just wanted to make sure they weren't leaving any money on the table.

No matter the situation, no matter how you look at it, no matter your motivation, when you choose to discount your fee, you are choosing to work harder to make less.

If you're going to make this decision, make it consciously. The fee you charge ripples out in so many different ways and on so many different levels. Remember, when a discount is the only way to win a client, they're probably a bad client who's going to take up the space of two good, full fee clients.

And while you might think this is an isolated incident, it's not. When you discount this deal, you're also likely to be discounting any future deals or referrals from this client. Plus, you make it easier to justify discounting in other situations. Is that the way you want to run your business?

Like I said before, it's easier to do something 100 percent of the time than 98 percent of the time. Six percent, no exceptions.

## COMMISSION CONVERSATIONS WITH
## TACTICAL EMPATHY

Over many years, I developed what I thought was the perfect commission conversation script. With flawless facts, logic, and reason, it led the prospect to the inevitable conclusion that it would be worth paying 6 percent to get the best possible results. It worked pretty well—better than anything else I'd ever seen.

I threw it in the trash when I met Chris, and have never gone back.

The conversation you need to have is not about facts, logic, and reason. It's about making the other person feel understood. When you apply Tactical Empathy to the commission dialogue, everything changes.

Imagine approaching that conversation with no fear. You're not here to convince anyone. They either want you in their corner or they don't, and you're here to find out.

So, you cross the street and look at the world from their perspective. You reach into their head, read their mind and heart, and get into alignment.

Then, you put the subject out on the table without hesitation. You demonstrate absolute confidence in your very presence. You're not afraid, and they know you will walk. They understand your fee is your fee, and if they want to work with you, that's the number.

Imagine showing up this way every time.

How empowering would that feel? How energizing would that be? What would that inspire inside of you?

How excited would you be to work with people who valued you, respected you, and above all, trusted you?

That's exactly where you'll end up if you apply everything you're learning in this book.

In your mind, this is probably a very big mountain to climb, if not an impossible one. Every part of your ego construct and all of your survival instincts are going to push back hard on this thought. Probably every word in this chapter feels like a suicide mission…but every great experience you have in life is found on the other side of your fears.

Let's break down exactly how to get there. The conversation is always situational, so when you use this framework, always remember to listen closely to the other person, and respond to what's happening in front of you.

## 1. Prepare your mindset.

Just as with every tough conversation we've talked about in this book, you need to approach it from a place of courage, curiosity, and confidence. Before you enter this situation, take the time to write out what the other person is probably thinking and feeling. Acknowledge your own thoughts and feelings, then let them go. Prepare to focus your full attention on the other person, with the simple goal of discovering what's on their mind.

## 2. Bring up the issue gently but directly.

For most people, any conversation about money is an awkward one. When you bring it up, use your skills from Chapter 4 to soften the blow.

At the beginning of the chapter, Regina did this beautifully when she said, "I've got some things we need to talk about that could be deal breakers for you. This is going really well, but I might throw a wrench in the works with this information, so I'd like to put it on the table now. Would you be opposed?"

You don't have to use her words, but you do want to warn the other person that you're about to say something they might not like. Get their permission first.

> There are some reasons why you might not want to work with me. I'd like to tell you about them now in case they're deal breakers for you. Would you be opposed?

> Then, say it directly.

> I'm a full-service, full fee agent. I charge 6 percent, keep 3.5 percent, and give 2.5 percent to the buyer's agent.

## 3. Find out what they're thinking and feeling, and make them feel understood.

You want to see through their point of view, and understand why they think that way. It doesn't mean you agree, just that you understand where they're coming from. Once they feel understood, every interaction will become more open and honest.

Start with some labels to find out what results they care about most. Here are some examples:

> You're probably hoping to get top dollar.

> You don't want to leave any money on the table.

You would like to pay as little in commission as possible.

Then, use a no-oriented question to establish what matters to them in an agent.

Would it be wrong to assume you want to work with someone who is trustworthy, competent, and a straight shooter? Did I miss anything important?

## 4. Use calibrated and no-oriented questions to make them think deeply about the role of your fee in their decision.

Most people instinctively want to pay less, but haven't thought through the consequences of that choice. Use a few questions like these to help them engage in that thought process and articulate it to you.

How are you going to factor the commission into your decision-making process?

How are you going to factor the final sale price into your decision-making process?

Would it be crazy to think that at some level, there is a correlation between the fee an agent charges and the results they produce?

What are you willing to give up in return for a lower commission?

What would you need to hear to raise your level of comfort regarding my fee?

Would it be crazy to think that the skill an agent brings to the transaction is more important than the fee they charge?

Would it be crazy to think the fee an agent charges is a direct reflection of their ability to negotiate?

THE FULL FEE AGENT

Would it be unreasonable to think that an agent who discounts their fee is giving you a real clue as to their ability to negotiate?

Would it be crazy to think that an agent's ability to negotiate is going to directly impact the final sales price of your home?

Would you be surprised to know that the final sales price of your home can vary 1 to 10 percent or more, up or down, based on your agent's ability to negotiate?

Would it be unreasonable to think the agent who produces a superior result is going to charge more?

Would it be wrong to think what you really want is to net more at the close of escrow?

What are the terms that would make you happy and allow us to go forward right now?

## 5. Share a story that will help them understand the choice they're facing.

Instead of shoving your track record in their face as evidence of your value, ask permission to share a story that illustrates how an agent can affect the results that matter most to the other person.

This is your opportunity to bend their reality. Change the loss they're focused on: not what am I paying but what could I lose if I choose the wrong agent? Are they willing to risk a $1 million difference in sale price over $20,000 in fees?

You're not trying to convince them, just putting the story out there for them to interpret in their own way. To do that, use a question like this:

Would you be opposed to going through a couple of real life scenarios that illustrate how commission and the final sales price actually impact what you net at the close of escrow?

Are you opposed to hearing why the discount agents can charge so much less and still claim to provide the same results or better?

## 6. Summarize the choice they're facing and put the ball in their court.

No convincing, no pressure, no fear. Just lay it out for them and let them decide.

What I share with every seller is that in the end, it comes down to who you want in your corner from start to finish. Who do you want guiding you, helping you navigate through the twists and turns of this process? Who do you want negotiating for you, fighting for every last dollar, making sure not to leave any money on the table? Most of all, who do you believe is going to put your interests first at all times, no matter what?

That's the person you hire, regardless of their fee. Do I think I am that person? Yes, but I'm probably a little biased. What's important is, do you think I am that person? If you do, let's work together. If you don't, let's shake hands, wish each other the best, and go our separate ways.

How would you like to proceed?

When you follow this framework, you open the door completely to being the Favorite or the Fool. If you're the Favorite, they're going to hire you there right on the spot. If not, they'll thank you and say they'll get back to you.

## 7. Address any pushback with proof of life questions.

You might not get a definitive answer immediately. Prospects sometimes push back, even if they do intend to hire you. They might say things like:

Is your fee negotiable?

Other agents are willing to do it for less.

We are really tight on money. We need every penny.

We have done a lot of business with you in the past. Can you give us a break going forward?

I can refer you business. Can you lower your fee?

I thought the going rate was _____?

Wow, that's a lot of money!!

If you sell the home to your own buyer, will you reduce your fee?

This is what we pay.

In the past, we have never paid more than _____ percent. And we have done a lot of business.

If we both buy and sell through you...will you give us a break on commission?

Do you offer a friends and family discount?

You are a small independent. Can't you be flexible?

(Developers) If we give you the listing on the back end, will you work for less on the purchase?

Instead of giving in or explaining why you can't, use a proof of life question to find out if they're serious about working with you. For example:

Why would you do business with me?

Why would you pay me 6 percent?

Why would you pay me more?

With all the other agents who are willing to work for less, why would you pay my full fee?

It seems like you are not opposed to the idea of working together...we just have to come to terms regarding commission.

Are you opposed to the idea of working with me, even though my fee is higher?

It sounds like you are not convinced you need to hire me in order to sell your home for top dollar.

It sounds like you have another agent in mind who charges less.

It sounds like someone else may be a better choice for you.

Are you totally and completely against the idea of working with me because my fee is higher?

If they can articulate why they want to do business with you, you're the Favorite, and they'll agree to your fee. If not, you're the Fool, and it's time to send them away in a limo.

Occasionally, you might even get pushback after a client hires you. For example, one of our coaching clients recently double-ended a $70 million listing. After the deal was done, the seller came back and asked for a 1 percent reduction in fee.

The agent was stunned. She knew she had done a great job, and sold the house at top dollar.

She called the seller and said, "I'm really sorry. I must have done a horrible job for you."

The seller replied, "No, you did an incredible job!"

So, the agent said, "Then I'm confused...it seems like I'm being punished."

That was all it took to get the seller to backtrack and happily accept the full fee.

## THE FEE OR THE FEELING

When it comes to commission, what is truly most important to a seller? Is it the fee you charge, or the feeling you give them in terms of how they are going to be taken care of in the transaction?

Once again, you must take your own feelings out of the equation. Most agents approach the commission discussion full of fear. If you do that, you'll try to convince the seller that you're the best person for the job, relying on facts, logic, and reason to persuade them of your value. You'll believe you need to tell them all the wonderful things you're going to do for them to justify why they should hire you.

This path leads you into the trap of making yourself a commodity. The more you share and explain, the less valuable you become in the eyes of the potential client you are speaking with. Remember: when you're explaining, you're losing.

Instead, your new approach is to turn the commission discussion into a conversation about trust. Rather than defending your fee, you're focusing on who the seller really wants to represent them. We broke that process down into steps in the last section. Here's how it sounds all together.

Seller: Why should I pay you more?

Agent: It's probably confusing that different agents charge different fees.

Seller: Yes, it is confusing.

Agent: Would it be wrong to assume that what you really want is to make sure you're not overpaying, and you're not leaving any money on the table?

Seller: That's right.

Agent: When it comes to selecting an agent to represent you in the sale of your home, I share this guidance with every potential seller...would you be opposed if I share it with you?

Seller: Please do.

Agent: When it comes to selecting your agent, choose the one who gives you the highest level of confidence in achieving the best outcome possible. Who you believe will best prepare and position you for success... Who you believe will best help you navigate through the selling process from start to finish...Who you believe will best protect your interests at all times. That is the person you want to hire, regardless of their fee.

Just like that, you've moved this dialogue from a number to a feeling.

If you're the Favorite, the door is wide open for them to choose you in that moment. More than anything else, the commission discussion revolves around whether you're the Favorite or the Fool...and that comes down to a feeling of trust.

## This Is Your Moment of Truth

As Steven Ross said, "Paying my full fee is the litmus test for having a great client."

Your commission is the cornerstone of your business. When you set your standard at 6 percent and stick to it fearlessly, everything else you've learned in this book must follow. It's impossible to uphold that standard successfully unless you practice everything else you've learned about Tactical Empathy. The 6 percent fee forces you to commit to that practice 100 percent.

You may have other standards you want to uphold in your business. For example, Regina always has her clients stage their homes and price to sell quickly. She also doesn't work Saturdays or answer the phone after 6 p.m. That's what it takes to run her business and life the way she wants, and it's nonnegotiable.

But, she doesn't have to have a tough conversation about each of those things. If she can get past the commission issue with a prospect, she knows they'll accept those things. If she can't, it doesn't matter.

The same is true for you. Set standards for how you work so that your business actually serves you and creates the life you want. Lay them out up front, just as Regina did. Just like your commission, those are reasons someone might not want to work with you.

But by far, the commission is the most important of all the standards. If a prospect agrees to that, they'll agree to it all.

That's why this whole chapter has focused exclusively on this one issue. Becoming a full-service, full fee agent is the culmination of everything you've learned in this book. It requires you to make the switch from transactions to relationships, from explaining your value to building trust, and from convincing to making people feel understood.

# KEY TAKEAWAYS

→ Everything you've learned so far comes together in the most important discussion you'll have with any client: the commission conversation.

→ If you're the Favorite, they'll agree to your fee. If you're not, it doesn't matter what your fee is—they probably won't hire you anyway.

→ There are all kinds of excuses for giving discounts, but none of them hold water. You and your clients are both better off if you stick to the standard of 6 percent, no exceptions.

→ Typical scripts for this conversation use facts, logic, and reason to try to convince the prospect of your worth. Throw them in the trash. Instead, use what you've learned about Tactical Empathy to lay out the issue and guide their decision.

→ This is your moment of truth, where you either challenge yourself to become a full-service, full fee agent with a business built on trust...or you get stuck in the status quo.

# CONCLUSION

*It's time to get your humanity—*
*and your life—back.*

CONGRATULATE YOURSELF! YOU'VE MADE IT ALL THE WAY TO THE end of this book, which means you were open-minded enough and value yourself enough to consider a new way of doing things. It probably seemed insane at first. Certainly, most of the things you've learned go completely against what agents typically do, and there are plenty of people who would tell you you're crazy to try this.

Hopefully, you've been paying close enough attention to realize by now that while it may be scary to change, it's the sanest decision you will ever make. To quote Frank Zappa, "Without deviation from the norm, progress is not possible."

Before, you were turning yourself into a commodity. You spent all your time chasing clients, convincing them to do what you want, and pushing everyone to close the deal. Chase, convince, close, over and over in a never-ending cycle of fear, attachment, hope, and disappointment.

THE FULL FEE AGENT

In your eagerness for more clients, more revenue, more prestige, more everything...you made yourself a slave to the transaction.

It's time to get your humanity—and your life—back.

It starts with recognizing how people actually think and make decisions. We're not machines who see the world without bias and weigh all the pros and cons mathematically. We're human beings with feelings and brains that have evolved to keep us alive, not to be unbiased. If there's one thing about human nature you always remember, let it be this: you can't overcome emotion with fact, logic, and reason.

Because of that, and because there's no such thing as an open mind, you've completely transformed the way you approach prospects. There is no convincing anyone to hire you—their minds are already made up. All you have to do is find out whether you're the Favorite or the Fool. When you use Tactical Empathy to make them feel understood, they'll reveal the answer to you. Instead of spending days on a listing appointment, you figure out within half an hour whether you really have a shot. If not, you happily walk away and save your time for the people who *want* to work with you.

Now, in every client relationship, you have a new focus: building trust. Gone are the days of explaining your value and giving away your time, effort, and money to win people over. You know now that the indirect route is faster. By building trust, you pave the way for every future interaction to be easier, more productive, and more joyful. All you have to do is let go of your own feelings and desires, then focus your complete attention on the other person. It's that simple.

You're not scared of tough conversations anymore, either. You used to avoid or sugarcoat them, but that just undermined your clients' trust in you. Now, you call out the negatives and break bad news as soon as possible, gently and with confidence. You've learned how to brace them for it and use Accusations Audits to make them feel understood. You've also used Accusations Audits to examine your own feelings and set them aside, so you can focus on the other person.

You've also stopped taking on responsibility for things that are outside your control. Before, you felt like it was your job to steer every choice and solve every problem. Now, you recognize that in the end, only the client can decide anything. Your job is just to be the trusted advisor who provides all the information they need to make informed, empowered choices. Your stress, angst, and frustration don't help—they just get in the way. So, you let it go and focus on guiding the client's decisions, not owning them.

To do that effectively, you've learned to start with no instead of pushing for yes. People hate to say yes—it makes them feel vulnerable and puts them on guard. Saying no, on the other hand, protects them and preserves their autonomy. After they say no, they're more open to hearing what you have to say. So, to guide your client, you begin with no-oriented questions. Then, you use calibrated (how and what) questions to help them think through tough issues and share what they truly want and don't want.

You've learned to use these Tactical Empathy techniques all the time, from the beginning of the relationship to the end—especially the end. The last impression is the lasting impression, and people who walk away feeling good about you are more likely to come back and refer other people to you. That's exactly what you need to build a sustainable business. So, you follow the Oprah Rule: send everyone away in a limo, no matter what.

All of this comes together in one single moment of truth: the commission conversation. It's the most important conversation you have with your clients, and the one that agents dread the most...but not you, because now you're a full-service, full fee agent. Your standard is 6 percent, and you stick to it 100 percent of the time. It's not because you're greedy. It's because charging 6 percent forces you to do everything else you've learned in this book. It challenges you to be the best agent you can be every day, and it rewards you with a business that's a joy instead of a drain on your life.

This book is not about following a series of steps to get what you want. It's about showing up as a human being who's here to serve other human beings, with no other agenda. You don't have to be a real estate machine who sacrifices their personal life and happiness to do business. You can be authentic and real, and *that's* the way to do more business in way less time, with way less stress. Instead of just surviving, you can start living your highest and best.

Remember, how you do business is more important than how much business you do. When you focus on the *how*, the score will take care of itself.

## START BY LETTING GO

I've said it over and over in this book, and I'll say it again: your feelings and desires have no place here. They are getting in your way. Start by letting them go.

You've been conditioned your whole life to believe that if you want something good to happen, you have to make it happen. You have to convince people to follow you and fight against everything that blocks your path. It's a constant battle between you and the universe, and you must get your way.

As Michael Singer put it in his book, *The Surrender Experiment*:

> The battle between individual will and the reality of life unfolding around us ends up consuming our lives. When we win the battle, we are happy and relaxed; when we don't, we're disturbed and stressed. Since most of us only feel good when things are going our way, we are constantly attempting to control everything in our lives.

That is not a peaceful existence. You spend all your time fighting to get what you think you need to be happy, but it's *the fight itself* that's killing your happiness.

With this book, you've learned how to stop fighting.

You're not here to make something happen. Instead, you show up, giving your highest and best to *what is* happening. How many times have you read those words already? If you take them to heart, it will take all the stress and struggle out of your work. Your business will transform from something that drains your life force to something that brings you joy and peace.

None of this is just about business either. Humans are humans, and our minds work the same in business and in our personal lives. Every single thing you've learned can apply just as well to your spouse, your kids, your parents, or your friends as it does to your clients. Tactical Empathy can transform all your relationships, if you let it.

## THREE THINGS TO MASTER

Tactical Empathy is a learned skill, and to start using it in your business, your habits have to change. If you're like most of the agents we coach, you're used to winging your client conversations and getting by on personality. That's not going to cut it anymore.

Replacing old habits with new ones takes deliberate practice. If you let yourself wing it, you'll default to your old ways and never make progress.

We've hit you with a lot of new skills in this book, and we don't expect you to master them all at once. These are the three you need to start with. The conversation hasn't really begun until these three things happen.

### 1. Prepare.

Get in the habit of taking time each day to anticipate upcoming conversations and write down what the other person will likely be thinking and feeling. Then, write down what you're thinking and feeling, including all your hopes and fears about the outcome of the conversation... and let them go. They don't matter, and they will only get in your way.

Whatever the interaction is—talking to a prospect, hosting an open house, writing an offer—prepare your mind to focus on the other person.

## 2. Read the situation.

Your old habit was to show up ready to push your agenda. Instead, you need to show up ready to read the other person. Focus exclusively on them and pay attention to the details—not just what they're saying but also their body language, tone of voice, and what they're *not* saying. Preparation makes this easier because it helps you know what to look for, just as reading scouting reports helped me read the situation on the field when I was in the NFL.

## 3. Make them feel understood.

Your only goal is to get them to say "that's right." Use mirrors and labels to elicit more information and confirm your understanding until you sense that emotional click, when you get in alignment with them. That's how you know you've successfully crossed to their side of the street and seen the world from their perspective.

## IT'S HARD...UNTIL IT'S NOT

I have a coaching client who is supposed to do expired listing calls every day, as part of his prospecting plan. He never does it, and every time we talk about it, he dreads it more and more.

Every day you don't do something, it gets harder. But when you let go of your excuses and just do it, it keeps getting easier.

I'll give you an extreme example from my personal life. A while back, I got a Peloton and pledged to ride it every single day. I started at five or ten miles a day and worked my way up to sixty.

Then, I thought: what if I rode one hundred miles a day for one hundred days?

It knew it would be hard at first. I had only ridden one hundred miles twice, once back in my twenties, and once on the Peloton a few months prior. But, I wanted to know how riding one hundred miles would feel after I had done it one hundred times.

Instead of approaching it with unhelpful thoughts and feelings about what I expected (*This is going to be so hard...I'm not sure I have the energy for this today...I'm already sore from yesterday...blah, blah, blah*), I got on the bike each day with an attitude of surrender.

I had made the commitment. I had no choice but to be there, on that bike, riding one hundred miles. I wasn't there to make something happen, but to discover what would happen. How would it feel to ride one hundred miles today?

Day one? Not so bad. Day two? Not so bad. Day three? Same thing.

By the time I had done it ten times, it was easy. There was no question I could do it.

That's what I'm asking you to do with Tactical Empathy. Commit to the decision to do it, and surrender to that commitment. Just do it —feel the fear, let it go, and do it anyway. There's a big difference between wondering if you can do it and working to get better. The first is a never-ending trap. The second lets you feed off the progress.

Forming new habits means building new neural pathways and using them over and over. The more you use them, the stronger they get, and the more your old pathways atrophy. When the new ones are stronger than the old ones, you have a new habit.

To make this happen, you've got to put in the reps.

Find low-stakes situations where you can practice these skills without taking big risks. Role play with your colleagues. Apply them in your personal life. At an open house, pick one label and use it on everyone who comes in, and practice reading whether they're a serious buyer or not.

When I first started practicing Tactical Empathy, I had to really think about it every time, and it felt unnatural. I just kept at it, and the awkwardness dissipated. Now, my brain is totally rewired, and it's almost effortless.

But it doesn't take years to get comfortable with this. Most of the time, it only takes a few reps to tip the balance from awkward and painful to exciting and fun.

For example, Chris has a technique based on Tactical Empathy for getting free upgrades at hotels. When he traveled for the first time after the COVID shutdown, he was reluctant to use it, even though he knew it was effective.

Unhelpful thoughts and feelings were running through his mind: *I don't have the energy for this...I'm out of practice...It probably won't work anyway.*

But he surrendered to his commitment to Tactical Empathy and did it anyway. It's just three simple steps:

1. "I'm getting ready to ruin your whole day." Brace the concierge for bad news.
2. "I know I'm about to sound like a self-centered, demanding

traveler who is so self-involved that they want something for nothing." Do a quick Accusations Audit.

3. "How much trouble will you get in if you give me a free upgrade to a suite?" Use a calibrated question to make them think about your request from a fresh perspective. The answer is usually none, which makes them happy to do it.

It worked. In fact, it worked at eight out of the nine hotels he stayed in on that trip, and it only failed in a hotel where all the rooms were suites anyway. After the fourth time, he no longer felt even the slightest internal resistance to doing it.

Give yourself at least four tries. By the fourth rep, it will feel noticeably easier than the first time. That's enough motivation to keep you going to the tenth rep, and the twentieth, and the hundredth, until you've lost count and it's just how you do business.

## LET YOURSELF TRANSFORM

Most agents have figured out how to do business. They just haven't figured out how to do business *and* have a life.

When my coaching clients start practicing Tactical Empathy and experiencing the results, they start asking a whole new set of questions. *I have all this time...what do I do? Can I really just relax and watch Netflix? Should I get a hobby? Get a dog? Start dating again?*

If you're one of the many, *many* real estate agents who has let your business take over your entire life, this will be you. It might sound funny when you read it, but this is serious stuff. These people are finally confronting the question: If I'm not just my business, who am I? Why am I here? What am I doing with my life?

That's how deep this really goes.

Tactical Empathy is not just another way to marginally improve your business results and go on your merry way. It is transformational. It changes everything: your relationships, your business, and your entire life.

We challenge you to *let it change you.*

Just like the clients who come to me for coaching, you picked up this book because you know you can do better. You know deep down that you're not a commodity; you're more than your production, and your clients are more than a paycheck.

You're a human being, here to serve other human beings.

For Further Negotiation Training Please Visit The Black Swan Group at www.blackswanltd.com.

# ACKNOWLEDGMENTS

## FROM STEVE SHULL

As a former professional football player, every year I look forward to the NFL Hall of Fame induction ceremonies. I love listening to the speeches given by each new gold jacket recipient, and what I love most is how each new Hall of Fame member says thank you to all the people in their lives that have made this accomplishment possible. Unfortunately, I am never going into the NFL Hall of Fame. However, in writing this book with my coauthor Chris Voss, I am now getting my chance to say thank you and acknowledge all the people who have influenced me greatly along my life journey.

First, I want to start with Chris Voss. As I share in the following pages, reading Chris's book *Never Split The Difference* was a real game changer for me. The moment I read the book, I knew I had to reach out to Chris, and the book you are about to read is the byproduct of all the work we have done together over the past five years. I thank you, Chris, and I know all my clients thank you as well.

And speaking of clients, I want to make a huge shout out to a very select group of coaching clients who have supported me and believed in me and worked with me for a very long time. All my clients are valuable and important to me, however this group has a very special place in my heart and mind: Vickey England, Terri and David Elston, Elaine Stucy (who wrote the forward), Stephanie Younger, Sally Forster Jones, Linda May, Jeffrey and Nadia Saad, Regina Vannicola, Mark Javonovich and Scott Hustis, and Dana Green and Santiago Arana. You are my Hall of Fame clients, and it has been the greatest privilege to work with each of you.

Another group of special people I want to thank include my football coaches: Pal Allison (high school); Lou Tepper, Wally Ake, and Jim Root (college); and Steve Crosby, Bill Arnsbarger, and Don Shula (professional). All of these men believed in me and taught me lessons I use every day in my coaching practice and life.

The following individuals have also been important teachers and mentors in my life, directly and indirectly: Pete Certo, David Allen, Fred Wilson, Betty Graham, Larry Kendall, Robert Reffkin, Ryan Holiday, Patrick Sweeny, and Michael Singer. Your wisdom is greatly appreciated.

And since I am not sure when I will get this chance again, I would like to make a heartfelt mention of my early childhood heroes: Johnny Callison, Wilt Chamberlain, Arnold Palmer, and Muhammad Ali. All of you stoked my imagination in a very significant way.

Next is my best friend in life, Jamie Leder: You have always been by my side, no matter what. I love you, man.

To Madison Fitzpatrick: I hope you know this book wouldn't have gotten written without you. THANK YOU!!

To Danielle Lazier and Sean McGlynn: thank you for being the pioneers and early adopters of this new methodology.

To my Dad: I was probably way too tough on you in life, but I always realized you were my biggest cheerleader.

To my mom: thank you for always reminding me and challenging me to be better.

To my brother and sister: The journey is not over yet. Let's all stay open to what's next.

To my incredible daughters, Sophia and Sasha: Talk about keeping a man honest! You are my heartbeat and my touchstone. I love you both so dearly, and hopefully you know you are a big part of this book.

Finally, to the love of my life, my wife Katerina: Without your never-ending support and encouragement (code for your foot up my ass), none of what I do is possible. You are my coach, and I love you for it!

## FROM CHRIS VOSS

This book would not have been possible without Brandon Voss and the entire Black Swan Group team. Brandon met Steve and told me, "You have to talk with this guy. We should work with him." He was right. Then, the entire Black Swan Group team, Vannessa Bernal in particular, kicked into gear and supported all our efforts. If you want to go fast, go alone. If you want to go far, go as a team. Thank you, Team Black Swan!

# ABOUT THE AUTHORS

**STEVE SHULL** is a former linebacker for the Miami Dolphins. When an injury forced him to change his game—literally—he pivoted into finance, then real estate, and found his calling when he started coaching other agents. Twenty-three years later, he read a book by Chris Voss, tossed out his playbook, and redesigned the whole program from scratch.

**CHRIS VOSS** served as the lead international kidnapping negotiator for the FBI. His business negotiation book *Never Split the Difference* has sold millions of copies around the world. After twenty-four years with the Bureau, he founded The Black Swan Group to help realtors, companies, and individuals take their negotiation skills to the next level.

# DEMONIALITY

# DEMONIALITY

## OR

## INCUBI AND SUCCUBI

### A Treatise

*Wherein is shown that there are in existence on earth rational creatures besides man, endowed like him with a body and a soul, that are born and die like him, redeemed by our Lord Jesus-Christ, and capable of receiving salvation or damnation.*

(17th century)

## REV. FATHER SINISTRARI OF AMENO

*Published from the original Latin manuscript discovered in London in the year 1872, and translated into French by Isidore Liseux*

QUICK TIME PRESS

Publisher's Cataloging-In-Publication Data

Rev. Father Sinistrari of Ameno, translated by Isidore Liseux
Demonality: Inccubi and Succubi: A Book of Demonology / Rev. Father Sinistrari of Ameno, translated by Isidore Liseux; Sinistrari of Ameno, Rev. Father, translated by Liseux, Isidore

Paperback    ISBN-13: 978-1-946774-62-0  ISBN-10: 1-946774-62-6
Hardback    ISBN-13: 978-1-946774-63-7  ISBN-10: 1-946774-63-4
Ebook    ISBN-13: 978-1-946774-64-4  ISBN-10: 1-946774-64-2

1. Religion; 2. Demonology. I Rev. Father Sinistrari of Ameno. II. Demoniality: Incubi and Succubi.

1. Body, Mind & Spirit; 2. Ancient Mysteries & Controversial Knowledge. I Rev. Father Sinistrari of Ameno. II. Demoniality: Incubi and Succubi.

1. Body, Mind & Spirit; 2. Unexplained Phenomena. I Rev. Father Sinistrari of Ameno. II. Demoniality: Incubi and Succubi.

REL100000 / OCC031000 / OCC023000 / OCC029000

# CONTENTS

DEMONIALITY 1

APPENDIX 40

PROOF OF DEMONIALITY 41

ABOUT THE AUTHOR 43

# DEMONIALITY

1. The first author who, to my knowledge, invented the word *Demoniality* is John Carmuel, in his *Fundamental Theology*, and before him I find no one who distinguished that crime from *Bestiality*. Indeed, all Theological Moralists, following in the train of S. Thomas (2, 2, question 154), include, under the specific title of *Bestiality*, "*every kind of carnal intercourse with anything whatever of a different species*" : such are the very words used by S. Thomas. Cajetanus, for instance, in his commentary on that question, classes intercourse with the Demon under the description of Bestiality; so does Sylvester, *de Luxuria*, Bonacina, *de Matrimonio*, question 4, and others.

2. However, it is clear that in the above passage, S. Thomas did not at all allude to intercourse with the Demon. As shall be demonstrated further on, that intercourse cannot be included in the very particular species of *Bestiality*; and, in order to make that sentence of the holy Doctor tally with truth, it must be admitted that when saying of the unnatural sin, "*that committed through intercourse with a thing of different species, it takes the name of Bestiality*", S. Thomas, by *a thing of different species*, means a living animal, of another species than man: for he could not here use the word *thing* in its most general sense, to mean indiscriminately an animate or inanimate being. In fact, if a man should fornicate *cum cadaver humano*, he would have to do with a thing of a species quite different from his own (especially according to the Thomists, who deny the form of human corporeity in a corpse); similarly *si cadaveri bestiali copularetur:* and yet, *talis coitus* would not be bestiality, but pollution. What therefore S. Thomas intended here to specify with preciseness, is carnal intercourse with a living thing of a species different from man, that is to say, with a beast, and he never in the least thought of intercourse with the Demon.

3. Therefore, intercourse with the Demon, whether Incubus or Succubus (which is, properly speaking, *Demoniality*), differs in kind from Bestiality, and does not in connexion with it form one very particular species as Cajetanus wrongly gives it; for, whatever may have said to the contrary some Ancients, and later Caramuel in his *Fundmental Theology*, unnatural sins differ from each other most distinctly. Such at least is the general doctrine, and the contrary opinion has been condemned by Alexander VII: first, because each of those sins carries with itself its peculiar and distinct disgrace, repugnant to chastity and to human generation; secondly, because the commission thereof entails each time the sacrifice of some good by its nature attached to the institution of the venereal act, the normal end of which is human generation; lastly, because they each have a different motive which in itself is sufficient to bring about, in divers ways, the deprivation of the same

1

good, as has been clearly shown by Fillucius, Crespinus and Caramuel.

4. It follows that Demoniality differs in kind from Bestiality, for each has its peculiar and distinct disgrace, repugnant to chastity and human generation. Bestiality is connexion with a living beast, endowed with its own peculiar senses and impulses; Demoniality, on the contrary, is copulation with a corpse (according at least to the general doctrine which shall be considered hereafter), a senseless and motionless corpse which is but accidentally moved through the power of the Demon. Now, if fornication with the corpse of a man, a woman, or a beast differs in kind from Sodomy and Bestiality, there is the same difference with regard to *Demoniality*, which, according to general opinion, is the intercourse of man with a corpse accidentally set in motion.

5. Another proof: in sins against nature, the unnatural semination (which cannot be regularly followed by generation) is a genus; but the object of such semination is the difference which marks the species under the genus. Thus, whether semination takes place on the ground, or on an inanimate body, it is pollution; if *cum homine in vase proepostero*, it is Sodomy; with a beast, bestiality: crimes which unquestionably all differ from each other in species, just as the ground, the corpse, the man and the beast, passive objects *talis seminationis*, differ in species from each other. But the difference between the Demon and the beast is not only specific, it is more than specific: the nature of the one is corporeal, of the other incorporeal, which makes a generic difference. Whence it follows that *seminationes* practiced on different objects differ in species from each other: and that is substantiated.

6. It is also a trite doctrine with Moralists, established by the Council of Trent, session 14, and admitted by Theologians, that in confession it suffices to state the circumstances which alter the species of sins. If therefore Demoniality and Bestiality belonged to the same very particular species, it would be enough that, each time he has fornicated with the Demon, the penitent should say to his confessor: *I have been guilty of the sin of Bestiality*. But that is not so: therefore those two sins do not both belong to the same very particular species.

7. It may be urged that if the circumstances of a sensual intercourse with the Demon should be revealed to the Confessor, it is on account of its offense against Religion, an offense which comes either from the worship rendered to the Demon, or from the homage or prayers offered up to him, or from the compact of fellowship entered into with him (*S. Thomas*, quest. 90). But, as will be seen hereafter, there are Incubi and Succubi to whom none of the foregoing applies, and yet *copula sequiter*. There is consequently, in that special case, no element of irreligion, no other character *quam puri et simplicis coitus*; and, if of the same species as *Bestiality*, it would be adequately stated by saying: *I have been guilty of the sin of Bestiality;* which is not so.

8. Besides, it is acknowledged by all Theological Moralist that *copula cum Daemon* is much more grievous than the same act committed with any beast soever. Now, in the same very particular species of sins, one sin is not more grievous than another; all are equally so: it comes to the same whether connection is had with a

bitch, an ass, or a mare; whence it follows that if *Demonality* is more grievous than Bestiality, those two acts are not of the same species. And let it not be argued, with Cajetanus, that *Demoniality* is more grievous on account of the offense to religion from the worship rendered to the Demon or the compact of fellowship entered into with him: as has been shown above, that is not always met with in the connection of man with Incubi and Succubi; moreover, if in the genus of unnatural sin *Demoniality* is more grievous than Bestiality, the offense to Religion is quite foreign to that aggravation, since it is foreign to that genus itself.

9. Now, having laid down the specific difference between *Demoniality* and Bestiality, so that the gravity thereof may be duly appreciated in view of the penalty to be inflicted (and that is our most essential object), we must inquire in how many different ways the sin of *Demoniality* may be committed. There is no lack of people who, infatuate with their small baggage of knowledge, venture to deny what has been written by the gravest authors and is testified by every day experience: namely, that the Demon, whether Incubus or Succubus, unites carnally not only with men and women, but also with beasts. They allege that it all comes from the human imagination troubled by the craft of the Demon, and that there is nothing in it but phantasmagoria and diabolical spells. The like happens, they say, to Witches or Sagas, who, under the influence of an illusion brought on by the Demon, fancy that they attend the nightly sports, dances, revels and vigils, and have carnal intercourse with the Demon, though in reality they are not bodily transferred to those places nor taking part in those deeds, as has been defined verbatim by a Capitule and two Councils.

10. Of course, it is not contested that sometimes young women, deceived by the Demon, fancy taking part, in their flesh and blood, in the nightly vigils of Witches, without its being anything but an imaginary vision. Thus, in a dream, one sometimes fancies *cum foemina alique concumbere, et semen vere excernitur, non tamen concubitus ille realis est*, but merely fantastic, and often brought about by a diabolical illusion: and here the above mentioned Capitule and Councils are perfectly right. But this is not always the case; on the contrary, it more often happens that Witches are bodily present at nightly vigils and have with the Demon a genuine carnal and corporeal connection, and that likewise Wizards copulate with the Succuba or female Demon. Such is the opinion of Theologians as well as of jurists, whose names will be found at length in the *Compendium Maleficarum*, or *Chronicle of Witches*, by Brother Francis Marie Guaccius. This doctrine if therein confirmed by eighteen instances adduced from the recitals of learned and truthful men whose testimony is beyond suspicion, and which proves that Wizards and Witches are indeed bodily present at vigils and most shamefully copulate with Demons, Incubi or Succubi. And, after all, to settle the question, we have the authority of S. Austin, who speaking of carnal intercourse between men and the Demon, expresses himself as follows, book 15th, chapt. 23rd of the *City of God*: "*It is widely credited, and such belief is confirmed by the direct or indirect testimony of thoroughly trustworthy people, that Sylvans and Fauns, commonly called Incubi, have frequently molested women, sought and obtained from them coition, There are*

*even Demons, whom the Gauls call Duses or Elfs, who very regularly indulge in those unclean practices: the fact is testified by so many and such weighty authorities, that it were impudent to doubt it."* Such are the very words of S. Austin.

11. Now, several authors profess, and it is confirmed by numerous experiments, that the Demon has two ways of copulating carnally with men or women: the one which it uses with Witches or Wizards, the other with men or women entirely foreign to witchcraft.

12. In the first case, the Demon does not copulate with Witches or Wizards until after a solemn profession, in virtue of which such wretched human beings yield themselves up to him. According to several authors who have related the judicial admissions of Witches when on the rack, and whose recitals have been collected by Francis-Marie Guaccisu, *Compend, Malef.*, book I, chapt. 7, that profession consists of eleven ceremonials:

13. Firstly, the Novices have to conclude with the Demon, or some other Wizard or Magician acting in the Demon's place, an express compact by which, in the presence of witnesses, they enlist in the Demon's service, he giving them in exchange his pledge for honours, riches and carnal pleasures.

14. Secondly, they abjure the catholic faith, withdraw from the obedience to God, renounce Christ and the protection of the most blessed Virgin Mary, and all the Sacraments of the Church.

15. Thirdly, they cast away the Crown, or Rosary of the most blessed Virgin Mary, the girdle of S. Francis, or the strap of S. Austin, or the scapular of the Carmelites, should they belong to one of those Orders, the Cross, the Medals, the *Agnus Dei*, whatever other holy or consecrated object may have been about their person, and trample them all under foot.

16. Fourthly, in the hands of the Devil they vow obedience and subjection: they pay him homage and vassalage, laying their fingers on some very black book. They bind themselves never to return to the faith of Christ, to observe none of the divine precepts, to do no good work, but to obey the Demon alone and, to attend diligently the nightly conventicles.

17. Fifthly, they promise to strive with all their power, and to give their utmost zeal and care for the enlistment of other males and females in the service of the Demon.

18. Sixthly, the Devil administers to them a kind of sacrilegious baptism, and after abjuring their Godfathers and Godmothers of the Baptism of Christ and Confirmation, they have assigned to them a new Godfather and a new Godmother, who are to instruct them in the arts of witchcraft; they drop their former name and exchange it for another, more frequently a scurrilous nickname.

19. Seventhly, they cut off a part of their own garments, and tender it as a token of homage to the Devil, who takes it away and keeps it.

20. Eighthly, the Devil draws on the ground a circle wherein stand the Novices, Witches and Wizards, and there they confirm by oath all their aforesaid promises.

21. Ninthly, they request the Devil to strike them out of the book of Christ, and to inscribe them in his own. Then comes forth that very black book on which, as has been said before, they laid hands when doing homage, and they are inscribed therein with the Devil's claw.

22. Tenthly, they promise the Devil sacrifices and offerings at stated times: once a fortnight or at least each month, the murder of some child, or an homicidal act of sorcery, and other weekly misdeeds to the prejudice of mankind, such as hailstorms, tempests, fires, cattle plagues, etc.

23. Eleventhly, the Demon imprints on them some mark, especially on those whose constancy he suspects. That mark, moreover, is not always of the same shape or figure: sometimes it is the image of a hare, sometimes a toad's leg, sometimes a spider, a puppy, a dormouse. It is imprinted on the most hidden parts of the body: with men, under the eye-lids, or the armpits, or the lips, on the shoulder, the fundament, or somewhere else; with women, it is usually on the breasts or the privy parts. Now, the stamp which imprints those marks is none other but the Devil's claw. This having been all performed in accordance with the instructions of the Teachers who have initiated the Novices, these promise lastly never to worship the Eucharist; to insult all Saints and especially the most blessed Virgin Mary; to trample under foot and vilify the holy images, the Cross and the relics of Saints; never to use the sacraments or sacramental ceremonials; never to make a full confession to the priest, but to keep always hidden from him their intercourse with the Demon. The Demon, in exchange, engages to give them always prompt assistance; to fulfill their desires in this world and to make them happy after their death. The solemn profession being thus performed, each has assigned to himself a Devil, called *Magiestellus* or Assistant Master, with whom he retires in private for carnal satisfaction; the said Devil being, of course, in the shape of a woman if the initiated person is a man, in the shape of a man, sometimes of a satyr, sometimes of a buck-goat, if it is a woman who has been received a witch.

24. If the authors be asked how it comes to pass that the Demon, who has no body, yet has carnal intercourse with man or woman, they unanimously answer that the Demon assumes the corpse of another human being, male or female as the case may be, or that, from the mixture of other materials, he shapes for himself a body endowed with motion, and by means of which he is united with the human being; and they add that when women are desirous of becoming pregnant by the Demon (which only occurs by the consent and express wish of the said women), the Demon is transformed into a Succuba, *et juncta homini semen ab eo recipit*; or else he procures pollution from a man during his sleep, *et semen prolectum in suo nativo calore, et cum vitali spritu conservat, et incubando foeminoe infert in ipsius matricem*, whence follows impregnation. Such is the teaching of Guaccius, book I, chapt. 12, who supports it on a number of quotations and instances taken from various Doctors.

25. At other times also the Demon, whether Incubus or Succubus, copulates with men or women from whom he receives none of the sacrifices, homage or offerings which he is wont to exact from Wizards or Witches, as aforesaid. He is

then but a passionate lover, having only one desire: the carnal possession of the loved ones. Of this there are numerous instances to be found in the authors, amongst which the case of Menippus Lycius, who, after frequent coition with a woman, was by her entreated to marry her; but a certain philosopher, who partook of the wedding entertainment, having guessed what that woman was, told Menippus that he had to deal with a *Compusa*, that is a Succuba Demon; whereupon the bride vanished bewailing: such is the narrative given by Coelius Rhodiginus, *Antiq.*, book 29, chapt. 5. Hector Boethius (*Hist. Scot.*) also relates the case of a young Scot, who, during many months, with closed doors and windows, was visited in his bed-room by a Succuba Demon of the most bewitching beauty; caresses, kisses, embraces, entreaties, she resorted to every blandishment *ut secum coiret*: but she could not prevail on the chaste young man.

26. We read likewise of numerous women incited to coition by the Incubus Demon, and who, though reluctant at first of yielding to him, are soon moved by his entreaties, tears and endearments; he is a desperate lover and must not be denied. And although this comes sometimes of the craft of some Wizard who avails himself of the agency of the Demon, yet the Demon not infrequently acts on his own account; and it happens not merely with women, but also with mares; if they readily comply with his desire, he pets them, and plaits their mane in elaborate and inextricable tresses; but if they resist, he ill-treats and strikes them, smites them with the glanders, and finally puts them to death, as is shown by daily experience.

27. A most marvelous and well-nigh incomprehensible fact: the Incubi whom the Italians call *Folletti*, the Spaniards *Duendes*, the French *Follets*, do no obey the Exorcists, have no dread of exorcisms, no reverence for holy things, at the approach of which they are not in the least overawed; very different in that respect from the Demons who vex those whom they possess; for, however obstinate those evil Spirits may be, however restive to the injunctions of the Exorcist who bids them leave the body they possess, yet, at the mere utterance of the most holy name of Jesus or Mary, or of some verses of Holy Writ, at the mere imposition of relics, especially of a piece of the wood of the Holy Cross, or the sight of the holy images, they roar at the mouth of the possessed person, they gnash, shake, quiver, and display fright and awe. But the Folletti show none of those signs, and leave off their vexations but after a long space of time. Of this I was an eye-witness, and shall relate a story which verily passes human belief: but I take God to witness that I tell the precise truth, corroborated by the testimony of numerous persons.

28. About twenty five years ago, when I was a lecturer on Sacred Theology in the convent of the Holy Cross, in Pavia, there was living in that city a married woman of unimpeachable morality, and who was most highly spoken of by all such as knew her, especially by the Friars; her name was Hieronyma, and she lived in the parish of S. Michael. One day, this woman had kneaded bread at home and given it out to bake. The oven-man brought her back her loaves when baked, and with them a large cake of a peculiar shape, and made of butter and Venetian paste, as is usual in that city. She declined to take it in, saying she had not made any thing of

6

the kind . "But," said the oven-man, "I had no other bread but yours to bake to-day, therefore this cake also must have come from your house; your memory is at fault." The good lady allowed herself to be persuaded, and partook of the cake with her husband, her little girl three years old, and the house servant. The next night, whilst in bed with her husband, and both asleep, she suddenly woke up at the sound of a very slender voice, something like a shrill hissing, whispering in her ears, yet with great distinctness, and inquiring whether "the cake had been to her taste?" The good lady, frightened, set about guarding herself with a sign of the cross and repeatedly calling the names of Jesus and Mary. "Be not afraid," said the voice, "I mean you no harm; quite the reverse: I am prepared to do anything to please you; I am captivated by your beauty, and desire nothing more than to enjoy your embraces." And she felt somebody kissing her cheeks, so lightly, so softly, that she might have fancied being grazed by the finest down. She resisted without giving any answer, merely repeating over and over again the names of Jesus and Mary, and crossing herself; the tempter kept on thus for nearly half an hour, when he withdrew.

The next morning the dame called on her Confessor, a discreet and learned man, who confirmed her in her faith, exhorted her to maintain her energetic resistance and to provide herself with some holy relics. On the ensuing nights, like temptation with the same language and kisses, like constancy also on the part of the woman. Weary however of such painful and persistent molestation, taking the advice of her Confessor and other grave men, she had herself exorcised by experienced Exorcists, in order to ascertain whether perchance she was not possessed. Having found in her no trace of the evil Spirit, they blessed the house, the bed-room, the bed, and enjoined on the Incubus to discontinue his molestations. All to no purpose: he kept on worse than ever, pretending to be love-sick, weeping and moaning in order to melt the heart of the lady, who however, by the grace of God, remained unconquered. The Incubus then went another way to work: he appeared in the shape of a lad or little man of great beauty, with golden locks, a flaxen beard that shone like gold, sea-green eyes calling to mind the flax-flower, and arrayed in a fancy Spanish dress. Besides he appeared to her even when in company, whimpering, after the fashion of lovers, kissing his hand to her, and endeavouring by every means to obtain her embraces. She alone saw and heard him: for everybody else, he was not to be seen.

The good lady kept persevering in her admirable constancy till, at last, after some months of courting, the Incubus, incensed at her disdain, had recourse to a new kind of persecution. First, he took away from her a silver cross filled with holy relics, and a holy wax or papal lamb of the blessed Pontiff Pius V, which she always carried on her person; then, leaving the locks untouched, he purloined her rings and other gold and silver jewelry from the casket wherein they were put away. Next, he began to strike her cruelly, and after each beating bruises and marks were to be seen on her face, her arms or other parts of her body, which lasted a day or two, then suddenly disappeared, the reverse of natural bruises which decreases slowly and by degrees. Sometimes, while she was nursing her little girl, he would snatch the child away from on her breast and lay it upon the rood, on the edge of the gutter, or hide it, but without ever harming it. Sometimes he would upset all the furniture, or smash to pieces saucepans, plates and other earthenware which, in the twinkling of an eye, he restored to their former state. One night that she was lying with her husband, the Incubus, appearing in his customary shape, vehemently urged his demand which she resisted as usual. The Incubus withdrew in a rage, and shortly came back with a large load of those flag stones which the Genoese, and the inhabitants of Liguria in general, use for roofing their house. With those stones he built around the bed a wall so high that it reached the tester, and that the couple could not leave their bed without using a ladder. This wall however was built up without lime; when pulled down, the flag were laid by in a corner where, during two days, they were seen by many who came to look at them; they then disappeared. On S. Stephen's day, the husband had asked some military friends to dinner, and, to do honour to his guests, had provided a substantial repast. Whilst they were, as customary, washing their hand before taking their seat, suddenly vanished the table dressed in the dining-room; all the dishes, saucepans, kettles, plates and crockery in the kitchen vanished likewise, as well as the jugs, bottles and glasses. You may imagine the surprise, the stupor of the guests, eight in number; amongst them was a Spanish Captain of infantry, who, addressing the company, said to them; "Do not be frightened, it is but a trick: the table is certainly still where it stood, and I shall soon find it by feeling for it." Having thus spoken, he paced round the room with outstretched arms, endeavouring to lay hold of the table; but when, after many circuitous perambulations, it was apparent that he labored in vain and grasped at nought but thin air, he was laughed at by his friends; and it being already high time for having dinner, each guest took up his cloak and set about to return home. They had already reached the street-door with the husband, who, out of politeness, was attending them, when they heard a great noise in the dining-room: they stood to ascertain the cause thereof, and presently the servant came up to announce that the kitchen was stocked with new vessels filled with food, and that the table was standing again in its former place. Having gone back to the dining-room, they were stupefied to see the table was laid, with cloths, napkins, salt-cellars, and trays that did not belong to the house, and with food which had not been cooked there. On a large sideboard all were arrayed in perfect order crystal, silver and gold chalices, with all kind of amphoras, decanters and cups filled with foreign wines, from the Isle of Crete, Campania, and the Canaries, the Rhine, etc. In the kitchen there was also an abundant variety of meats in saucepans and dishes that had never been seen there before. At first, some of the guests hesitated whether they should taste of that food; however, encouraged by others, they sat down, and soon partook of the meal, which was found exquisite. Immediately afterwards, as they were sitting before a seasonable fire, everything vanished at once, the dishes and the leavings, and in their stead reappeared the cloth of the house and the victual which had been previously cooked; but, for a wonder, all the guests were satisfied, so that no one thought of supper after such a magnificent dinner. A clear proof that the substituted viands were real and nowise fictitious.

This kinds of persecution had been going on some months, when the lady betook herself to the blessed Bernardine of Feltri, whose body is worshipped in the church of St James, a short distance from the walls of the city. She made a vow to him that she would wear, during a whole twelve-month, a grey frock, tied round her waist with a piece of cord, and such as is worn by the Minor Brethren, the order to which had belonged the blessed Bernardine; this she vowed, in the hope of being, through his intercession, at last rid of the persecution of the Incubus. And accordingly, on the 28th of September, the vigil of the Dedication of the Archangel S. Michael, and the festival of the blessed Bernardine, she assumed the votive robe. The next morning, which was S. Michael's festival, the afflicted woman proceeded to the church of St Michael, her own parish, already mentioned; it was about ten o'clock, a time when a crowd of people were going to mass. She was no sooner set foot on the threshold of the church, than her clothes and ornaments fell off to the ground, and disappeared in a gust of wind, leaving her stark naked. There happened fortunately to be among the crowd two cavaliers of mature age, who, seeing what had taken place, hastened to divest themselves of their cloaks with which they concealed, as well as they could, the woman's nudity, and having put her into a vehicle, accompanied her home. The clothes and trinkets taken by the Incubus were not restored by him before six months had elapsed.

I might relate many other most surprising tricks which that Incubus played on her, were it not wearisome. Suffice it to say that, for a number of years he persevered in his temptation of her, but that finding at last that he was losing his pains, he desisted from his vexatious importunities.

29. In the above case, as well as in others that may be heard or read of occasionally, the Incubus attempts no act against Religion; he merely assails chastity. In consequence, consent is not a sin through ungodliness, but through incontinence.

30. Now, it is undoubted by Theologians and philosophers that carnal intercourse between mankind and the Demon sometimes gives birth to human beings; that is how is to be born the Antichrist, according to some Doctors, such as Bellarmin, Suarez, Maluenda, etc. They further observe that, from a natural cause, the children thus begotten by Incubi are tall, very hardy and bold, very proud and wicked. Thus writes Maluenda; as for the cause, he gives it from Vallesius, Archphysician in Reggio: "What Incubi introduce in *uterus*, is not *qualcumque neque quantumcumque semen*, but abundant, very thick, very warn, rich in spirits and free from serosity. This moreover is an easy thing for them, since they have but to choose ardent, robust men, *et abundantes multo semine, quibus succumbant*, and then women of a like constitution, *quibus incumbant*, taking care that both shall enjoy *voluptatem solito majorem, tanto enim abundantius emittitur semen, quanto cum majori voluptate excernitur*." Those are the words of Vallesius, confirmed by Maluenda who shows, from the testimony of various Authors, mostly classical, that such associations gave birth to: Romulus and Remus, according to Livy and Plutarch; Servius-Tullius, the sixth

king of Rome, according to Dyonisius of Halicarnassus and Pliny the Elder; Plato the Philosopher, according to Diogenes Laertius and Saint Hieronymus; Alexander the Great, according to Plutarch and Quintus-Curtius; Seleucus, king of Syria, according to Justinus and Appianus; Scipio Africanus the Elder, according to Livy; the emperor Caesar Augustus, according to Suetonius; Aristomenes the Messenian, an illustrious Greek commander, according to Strabo and Pausanias; as also Merlin or Melchin the Englishman, born from an Incubus and a nun, the daughter of Charlemagne; and, lastly, as shown by the writings of Cochloeus quoted by Maluenda, that damned Heresiarch *ycleped* Martin Luther.

31. However, with due deference to so many and such learned Doctors, I hardly see how their opinion can bear examination. For, as Pererius truly observes in his *Commentary on the Genesis*, chapt. 6, the whole strength and efficiency of the human sperm reside in the spirits which evaporate and vanish as soon as issued from the genital vessels wherein they were warmly stored: all medical men agree on that point. It is consequently not possible that the Demon should preserve in a fit state for generation the sperm he has received; for it were necessary that whatever vessel he endearvoured to keep it in should be equally warm with the human genital organs, the warmth of which is nowhere to be met with but in those organs themselves. Now, in a vessel where that warmth is not intrinsical but extraneous, the spirits get altered, and no generation can take place. There is this other objection, that generation is a vital act by which man, begetting from his own substance, carries the sperm through natural organs to the spot which is appropriate to generation. On the contrary, in this particular case, the introduction of sperm cannot be a vital act of the man who begets, since it is not carried into the womb by his agency; and, for the same cause, it cannot be said that the man, whose sperm it was, has begotten the fetus which proceeds from it. Nor can the Incubus be deemed its father, since the sperm does not issue from his own substance. Consequentially, a child would be born without a father, which is absurd. Third objection: when the father begets in the course of nature, there is a concurrence of two casualties: the one, material, for he provides the sperm which is the matter of generation; the other, efficient, for he is the principal agent of generation, as Philosophers agree in declaring. But, in this case, the man who only provided the sperm would contribute but a mere material, without any action tending to generation; he could therefore not be regarded as the father of the child begotten under those circumstances; and this is opposed to the notion that the child begotten by an Incubus is not his son, but the son of the man whose sperm the Incubus has taken.

32. Besides, there is not a shadow of probability in what was written by Vallesius and quoted from him by us (*Vide supra no. 30*); and I wonder that anything so extravagant should have fallen from the pen of such a learned man. Medical men are well aware that the size of the fetus depends, not indeed on the quantity of matter, but on the quantity of virtue, that is to say of spirits held by the sperm; there lies the whole secret of generation, as is well observed by Michael Ettmuller, *Institut. Medic. Physiolog.* : "Generation," says he, "entirely depends upon the genital spirit

contained within an envelope of thicker matter; that spermatic matter does not remain in the uterus, and has no share in the formation of the fetus; it is but the genital spirit of the female, that permeates the pores, or, less frequently, the tubes of the uterus, which it fecundates by that means." Of what moment can therefore the quantity of sperm be for the size of the fetus? Besides, it is not always a fact that men thus begotten by Incubi are remarkable for the huge proportions of their body: Alexander the Great, for instance, who is said to have been thus born, as we have mentioned, was very short; as the poet said of him:

*Magnus Alexander corpore parvus erat.*

Besides, although it is generally a fact that those who are thus begotten excel other men, yet such superiority is not always shown by their vices, but sometimes by their virtues and even their morals; Scipio Africanus, for instance, Caesar Augustus and Plato the Philosopher, as is recorded of each of them respectively by Livy, Suetonius and Diogenes Laertius, had excellent morals. Whence may be inferred that, if other individuals begotten in the same way have been downright villains, it was not owing to their being born of an Incubus, but to their having, of their own free will, chosen to be such.

We also ready in the Testament, *Genesis*, chap. 6, verse 4, that giants were born when the sons of God came in unto the daughters of men: that is the very letter of the sacred text. Now, those giants were men of *great stature*, says *Baruch*, chap. 3, verse 26, and far superior to other men. Not only were they distinguished by their huge size, but also by their physical power, their plundering habits and their tyranny. Through their criminal excesses the Giants were the primary and principal cause of the Flood, according to Cornelius a Lapide, in his *Commentary on Genesisi.* Some contend that by Sons of God are meant the sons of Seth, and by Daughters of men the daughters of Cain, because the former practiced piety, religion and every other virtue, whilst the descendants of Cain were quite the reverse; but, with all due deference to Chrysostom, Cyrillus, Hilarius and others who are of that opinion, it must be conceded that it clashes with the obvious meaning of the text. Scripture says, in fact, that of the conjunction of the above mentioned were born men of huge bodily size: consequently, those giants were not previously in existence, and if their birth was the result of that conjunction, it cannot be ascribed to the intercourse of the sons of Seth with the daughters of Cain, who being themselves of ordinary stature, could but procreate children of ordinary stature. Therefore, if the intercourse in question gave birth to beings of huge stature, the reason is that it was not the common connection between man and woman, but the performance of Incubi Demons who, from their nature, may very well be styled sons of God. Such is the opinion of the Platonist Philosophers and of Francis Georges the Venetian; nor is it discrepant from that of Josephus the Historian, Philo the Jew, S. Justinus the Martyr, Clement of Alexandria, and Tertullian, who look upon Incubi as corporeal Angels who have allowed themselves to fall into the sin of lewdness with women. Indeed, as shall be shown hereafter, though seemingly distinct, those two opinions are but one and the same.

33. If therefore these Incubi, in conformity with general belief, have begotten Giants by means of sperm taken from man, it is impossible, as aforesaid, that of that sperm should have been born any but men of approximately the same size as he from whom it came; for it would be in vain for the Demon, when acting the part of a Succubus, to draw from man an unwonted quantity of prolific liquor in order to procreate therefrom children of higher stature; quantity has nothing to do here, since all depends, as we have said, upon the vitality of that liquor, not its quantity. We are therefore bound to infer that Giants are born of another sperm than man's, and that, consequently, the Incubus Demon, for the purpose of generation, uses a sperm which is not man's. But then, what is to be said?

34. Subject to correction by our Holy Mother Church, and as a mere expression of opinion, I say that the Incubus Demon, when having intercourse with women, begets the human fetus from his own sperm.

35. To many that proposition will seem heterodox and hardly sensible; but I beg of my reader not to condemn it precipitately; for if, as Celsus says, it is improper to deliver judgment without having thoroughly inquired into the law, no less unfair is the rejection of an opinion, before the arguments upon which it rests have been weighed and confuted. I have therefore to prove the above conclusion, and must necessarily premise with some statements.

36. Firstly, I premise, as an article of belief, that there are purely spiritual creatures, not in any way partaking of corporeal matter, as was ruled by the Council of Lateran, under the pontificate of Innocent III. Such are the blessed Angels, and the Demons condemned to ever-lasting fire. Some Doctors, it is true, have professed, subsequently even to this Council, that the spirituality of Angels and Demons is not an article of belief; others even have asserted that they are corporeal, whence Bonaventure Baron has drawn the conclusion that it is neither heretical nor erroneous to ascribe to Angels and Demons a twofold substance, corporeal and spiritual. Yet, the Council having formally declared it to be an article of belief that *God is the marker of all things visible and invisible, spiritual and corporeal, who has raised from nothing every creature spiritual or corporeal, Angelic or terrestrial,* I contend it is an article of belief that there are certain merely spiritual creatures, and that such are Angels; not all of them, but a certain number.

37. It may seem strange, yet it must be admitted not to be unlikely. If, in fact, Theologians concur in establishing amongst Angels a specific, and therefore essential, diversity so considerable that, according to St. Thomas, there are not two Angels of the same species, but that each of them is a species by himself, why should not certain Angels be most pure spirits, of a consequently very superior nature, and others corporeal, therefore of a less perfect nature, differing thus from each other in their corporeal or incorporeal substance? This doctrine has the advantage of solving the otherwise insoluble contradiction between two Ecumenical Councils, namely the Seventh General Synod and the abovementioned Council of Lateran.

For, during the fifth sitting of that Synod, the second of Nicea, a book was introduced written by John of Thessalonica against a pagan Philosopher, wherein occur the following propositions: "*Respecting Angels, Archangels and their Powers, to which I adjoin our own Souls, the Catholic Church is really of opinion that they are intelligences, but not entirely bodyless and senseless, as you Gentiles aver; she on the contrary ascribes to them a subtile body, aerial or igneous, according to what is written: He makes the spirits His Angels, and the burning fire His Minister.*" And further on: "*Although not corporeal in the same way as ourselves, made of the four elements, yet it is impossible to say that Angels, Demons and Souls are incorporeal; for they have been seen many a time, invested with their own body, by those whose eyes the Lord had opened.*" And after that book had been read through before all the Fathers in Council assembled, Tharasius, the Patriarch of Constantinople, submitted it to the approval of the Council, with these words: "*The Father showeth that Angels should be pictured, since their form can be defined, and they have been seen in the shape of men.*" Without a dissentient, the Synod answered: "*Yes, my Lord.*"

38. That this approbation by a Council of the doctrine set forth at length in the book of John establishes an article of belief with regard to the corporeity of Angels, there is not a shadow of doubt: so Theologians toil and moil in order to remove the contradiction apparent between that decision and the definition, above quoted, by the Council of Lateran. One of them, Suarez, says that if the Fathers did not disprove such an assertion of the corporeity of Angels, it is because that was not the question. Another contends that the Synod did approve the conclusion, namely that Angels might be pictured, but not the motive given, *their corporeity.* A third, Molina, observes that the definitions issued in Council by the Synod were thus issued only at the *seventh sitting,* whence he argues that those of the previous sittings are not definitions of belief. Others, lastly, write that neither the Council of Nicea nor that of Lateran intended defining a question of belief, the Council of Nicea having spoken according to the opinion of the Platonists, which describes Angels as corporeal beings and was then prevailing, whilst that of Lateran went with Aristoteles, who, in his 12th book of *Metaphysics,* lays down the existence of incorporeal intelligences, a doctrine which has since carried the day with most Doctors over Platonists.

39. But anyone can discern the invalidity of those answers, and Bonaventure Baro (*Scot. Defens.,* tome 9) proves to evidence that they do not bear. In consequence, in order to agree the two Councils, we must say that the Council of Nicea meant one species of Angels, and that of Lateran another: the former, corporeal, the latter on the contrary absolutely incorporeal; and thus are reconciled two otherwise irreconcilable Councils.

40. Secondly, I premise that the word Angel applies, not indeed to the kind, but to the office: the Holy Fathers are agreed thereupon (St. Ambrose, on the *Epistle to the Hebrews*; St. Austion, *City of God*; St. Gregory, *Homily 34 on Scripture*; St. Isidorus, *Supreme Goodness*). An Angel, very truly says St. Ambrose, is thus styled, not because he is a spirit, but on account of his office: Ἄγγελος in Greek, *Nuntius* in Latin, that is to say *Messenger;* it follows that whoever is entrusted by God with a mission, be

he spirit or man, may be called an Angel, and is thus called in the Holy Scriptures, where the following words are applied to Priests, Preachers and Doctors, who, as Messengers of God, explain to men the divine will (Malachi, chapt. 2, v. 7). *"The priest's lips should keep knowledge, and they should seek the law at his mouth, for he is the Angel of the Lord of Hosts."* The same prophet, chapt. 3, v. 1, bestows the name of Angel on St. John the Baptist, when saying: *"Behold, I will send my Angel and he shall prepare the way before me."* That this prophecy literally applies to St. John the Baptist is testified by our Lord Jesus-Christ, in the Gospel, according to St. Matthew, chapt. 11, v. 10. Still more: God himself is called an Angel, because he has been sent by His Father to herald the law of mercy. To witness, the prophecy of Isaiah, chapt. 9, v. 6, according to Septuagint: *"He shall be called an Angel of Wonderful Counsel."* And more plainly still in Malachi, chapt. 3, v. 1: *"The Lord whom ye seek shall suddenly come to his temple, even the Angel of the covenant whom ye delight in,"* a prophecy which literally applies to our Lord Jesus-Christ. There is consequently nothing absurd in the contention that some Angels are corporeal, since men, who assuredly have a body, are called Angels.

41. Thirdly, I premise that neither the existence nor the nature of the natural things in this world has been sufficiently investigated to allow of denying a fact, merely because it has never been previously spoken or written about. In the course of time have not new lands been discovered which the Ancients knew not of? New animals, herbs, plants, fruits and seeds, never seen elsewhere? And if that mysterious Austral land came at last to be explored, as has been to this day vainly tried by so many travelers, what unforeseen disclosures would be the result! Through the intervention of the microscope and other instruments used by modern experimental Philosophy, combined with the more exact methods of investigation of Anatomists, have there not been, and are there not, every, brought to light the existence, qualities and characteristics of a number of natural things unknown to ancient Philosophers, such as fulminating gold, phosphorus, and a hundred other chemical compounds, the circulation of the blood, the lacteal vessels, the lymphducts and other recent anatomical discoveries? To deride a doctrine because it does not happen to be mentioned in any ancient author would therefore be absurd, especially bearing in mind this axiom of Logic: *locus ab auctoritate negative non tenet.*

42. Fourthly, I premise that Holy Scripture and ecclesiastical tradition do not teach us anything beyond what is requisite for the salvation of the soul, namely Faith, Hope and Charity. Consequently, from a thing not being stated either by Scripture or tradition it must not be inferred that that thing is not in existence. For instance, Faith teaches us that God, by His Word, made things visible, and invisible, and also that, through the merits of our Lord Jesus-Christ, grace and glory are conferred on every rational creature. Now, that there be another World than the one we live in, and that it be peopled by men not born of Adam but made by God, in some other way, as is implied by those who believe the lunar globe to be inhabited; or further, that in the very World we dwell in, there be other rational creatures

14

besides man and the Angelic Spirits, creatures generally invisible to us and whose being is disclosed but accidentally, through the instrumentality of their own power; all that has nothing to do with Faith, and the knowledge or ignorance thereof is no more necessary to the salvation of man than knowing the number or nature of all physical things.

43. Fifthly, I premise that neither Philosophy nor Theology is repugnant to the possible existence of rational creatures having spirit and body and distinct from man. Such repugnance could be supported only on God, and that is inadmissible, since he is all-mighty, or on the thing to be made, and that likewise cannot be supported; for, as there are purely spiritual creatures, such as Angels, or merely material, such as the World, or lastly semi-spiritual and semi-corporeal, of an earthly and gross corporeity, such as man, so there may well be in existence a creature endowed with a rational spirit and a corporeity less gross, more subtle than man's. No doubt, moreover, but that after Resurrection, the souls of the blessed will be united with a glorious and subtle body; from which may be inferred that God may well have made a rational and corporeal creature whose body naturally enjoys the subtilty which will be conferred by the grace on the glorious body.

44. But, the possible existence of such creatures will be still better set forth by solving the arguments which can be adduced against our conclusion, and replying to the questions it may raise.

45. First question: should such creatures by styled rational animals? And if so, in what do they differ from man, with whom they would have that definition in common?

46. I reply: Yes, they would be rational animals, provided with senses and organs even as man; they would, however, differ from man not only in the more subtle nature, but also in the matter of their body. In fact, as is shown by Scripture, man has been made from the grossest of all elements, namely clay, a gross mixture of water and earth: but those creatures would be made from the most subtle part of all elements, or of one or other of them; thus, some would proceed from earth, others from water, or air, or fire; and, in order that they should not be defined in the same terms as man, to the definition of the latter should be added the mention of the gross materiality of his body, wherein he would differ from said animals.

47. Second question: At what period would those animals have been originated, and wherefrom? From earth, like the beasts, or from water, like quadrupeds, birds, etc.? Or, on the contrary, would they have been made, like man, by our Lord God?

48. I reply: It is an article of belief, expressly laid down by the Council of Lateran, that whatever is in fact and at present, was made in the origin of the world. By His all-mighty virtue, God, from the beginning of time, raised together from nothing both orders of creatures, spiritual and corporeal. Now, those animals also would be included in the generality of creatures. As to their formation, it might be said that God Himself, through the medium of Angels, made their body as he did man's, to which an immortal spirit was to be united. That body being of a nobler

nature than that of other animals, it was meet that it should be united to an incorporeal and highly noble spirit.

49. Third question: Would those animals descend from one individual, as all men descend from Adam, or, on the contrary, would many have been made at the same time, as was the case for the other living things issued from earth and water, wherein were males and females for the preservation of the kind by generation? Would there be amongst them a distinction between the sexes? Would they be subject to birth and death, to senses, passions, want of food, power of growth? If so, what their nutrition? Would they lead a social life, as men so? By what laws ruled? Would they build up cities for their dwellings, cultivate the arts and sciences, hold property, and wage war between themselves, as men are wont to?

50. I reply: It may be that all descend from one individual, as men descend from Adam; it may be also that a number of males and females were made initially, who preserved their kind by generation. We will further admit that they are born and die; that they are divided into males and females, and are moved by senses and passions, as men are; that they feed and grow according to the size of their body; their food, however, instead of being gross like that required by the human body, must be delicate and vapoury, emanating through spirituous effluvia from whatever in the physical world abounds with highly volatile corpuscles, such as the flavours of meats, especially of roasts, the fume of wine, the fragrancy of fruit, flowers, aromatics, which evolve an abundance of those effluvia until all their subtle and volatile parts have been completely evaporated. To their being able to lead a social life, with distinctions of rank and precedence; to their cultivating the arts and sciences, exercising functions, maintaining armies, building up cities, doing in short whatever is requisite for their preservation, I have in the main no objection.

51. Fourth question: What would their figure be, human or otherwise? Would the ordering of the divers parts of their body be essential, as with other animals, or merely accidental, as with fluid substances, such as oil, water, clouds, smoke, etc.? Would those organic parts consist of various substances, as is the case with the organs of the human body, wherein are to be found very gross parts, such as the bones, others less gross, such as the cartilages, and others slender, such as the membranes?

52. I reply: As regards their figure, we neither can nor should be affirmative, since it escapes our senses, being too delicate for our sight or our touch. That we must leave to themselves, and to such as have the privilege of intuitive acquaintance with immaterial substances. But, so far as probability goes, I say that their figure tallies with the human body, save some distinctive peculiarity, should the very tenuity of their body not be deemed sufficient. I am led to that by the consideration that of all the works of God the human frame is the most perfect, and that whilst all other animals stoop to the ground, because their soul is mortal, God, as Ovid, the poet, say, in his *Metamorphoses*,

*Gave man an erect figure, bidding him behold the heavens*

*And raise his face towards the stars,*

man's soul having been made immortal for the heavenly abode. Considering that the animals we are speaking of would be gifted with a spirit immaterial, rational and immortal, capable therefore of beatitude an damnation, it is proper to admit that the body to which that spirit is united may be like unto the most noble animal frame, that is to say to the human frame. Whence it follows that in the divers parts of that body there must be an essential order; that the foot, for instance, cannot be an appendage of the head, nor the hand to the belly, but that each organ is in its right place, according to the functions is has to perform. As to the constitutive parts of those organs, it is, in my opinion, necessary that there should be some more or less strong, others more or less slender, in order to meet the requirements of the organic working. Nor can this be fairly objected to on the ground of the slenderness of the bodies themselves; for the strength or thickness of the organic parts alluded to would not be absolute, but merely in comparison with the more slender ones. That, moreover, may be observed in all natural fluids, such as wine, oil, milk, etc.; however homogenous and similar to each other their component parts may look, yet they are not so; for some are clayish, other aqueous; there are fixed salts, volatile salts, brimstone, all of which are made obvious by a chemical analysis. So it would be in our case: for, supposing the bodies of those animals to be as subtle and slender as the natural fluids, air, water, etc., there would nevertheless be discrepancies in the quality of their constitutive parts, some of which would be strong when compared with others more slender, although the whole body which they compose might be called slender.

53. It may be objected that this repugnant to what was said above concerning the essential ordering of the parts among themselves; that it is seen that, in fluid and subtle bodies, one part is not essentially but only accidentally connected with another; that a part of wine, for instance, just now contiguous with some other, soon comes in contact with a third, if the vessel be turned upside down or the wine shaken, and that all the parts together exchange positions at the same time, though it be still the same wine. Whence it should be inferred that the bodies of those animals would have no permanent figure, and would consequently not be organic.

54. I reply that I deny the assumption. In fact, if in fluid bodies the essential ordering of the parts is not apparent, it subsists none the less, and causes a compound to preserve its own state. Wine, for instance, when expressed from the grapes, seems a thoroughly homogenous liquor, and yet is not so; for there are gross parts which, in the long run, subside in the casks; there are also slender parts which evaporate; fixed parts, such as tartar; volatile parts, such as brimstone and alcohol; others again, half volatile and half fixed, such as phlegm. Those divers parts do not respectively maintain an essential order; for no sooner has the must been expressed from the grapes, and been styled brimstone or volatile spirits, than

it continues so closely involved with the particles of tartar, which is fixed, as not to be in any way able to escape.

55. That is the reason why must recently expressed from the grapes is of no use for the distillation of the sulfurous spirits, commonly called *brandy*; but, after forty days fermentation, the particles of the wine change places: the spirits, no longer bound with the tartaric particles which they kept in suspension through their own volatility, whilst they were, in return, kept down by them and prevented from escaping, sever from those particles, and continue confused with the phlegmatic parts from which they become easily released by the operation of fire, and evaporate: thus, by means of distillation, brandy is made, which is nothing but the brimstone of wine volatilized by heat with the most slender part of phlegm. At the end of forty days another fermentation begins, which extends more or less, according as the maturity of the wine is more or less perfect, and the termination of which is dependent on the greater or lesser abundance of sulphurous spirits. If abounding with brimstone, the wine sours and turns to vinegar; if, on the contrary, it holds but little brimstone, it ropes, and becomes what the Italians call *vino molle* or *vino guasto*. If the wine is at once ripe, as happens in other cases, it sours or ropes in less time, as is shown by every day experience. Now, in said fermentation the essential order of the parts of wine is altered, but not so its quantity nor its matter, which neither changes nor decreases: a bottle that had been with wine is, after a certain time, found to be filled with vinegar, without any alteration in its quantity of matter; the essential order of its parts has alone been modified: the brimstone, which, as we have said, was united to the phlegm and separated from the tartar, becomes again involved and fixed with the tartar; so that, on distilling the vinegar, there issues from it first an insipid phlegm, and then spirits of vinegar, which are the brimstone of wine intermixed with particles of tartar that is less fixed. Now, the essential shifting of the aforesaid parts alters the substance of the juice of the grapes, as is clearly shown by the varied and contrary effects of must, wine, vinegar, and ropy or spoiled wine; for which cause the two first are fit, but the two last unfit materials for consecration. We have borrowed the above exposition of the economy of wine from the able work of Nicholas Lemery, perfumer to the King of France, *Course of Chemistry*, p. 2. c. q.

56. If now we apply that natural doctrine to our subject, I say that, being given the corporeity of the animals in question, subtle and slender like the substance of liquids; being given also their organization and figure, which demand an essential order of the various parts, an adverse supposition could raise no argument contrary to their existence; for, just as the jumbling together of the parts of wine and the diversity of their accidental dispositions do not alter their essential order, even so it would be with the slender frame of our animals.

57. Fifth question: Would those animals be subject to diseases and other infirmities under which mankind lies, such as ignorance, fear, idleness, sensual paralysis, etc.? Would they be wearied through labour, and require, for recruiting their strength, sleep, food, drink? And what food, what drink? Would they be fated to

die, and might they be killed casually, or by the instrumentality of other animals?

58. I reply: Their bodies, though subtle, being material, they would of course be liable to decay: they might therefore suffer from adverse agencies, and consequently be diseased; that is, their organs might not perform, or painfully and imperfectly perform the office assigned to them, for therein consist all diseases whatever with certain animals, as has been distinctly explained by the most illustrious Michael Ettmuller, *Physiology*, c. v. thesis 1. In sooth, their body being less gross than the human frame, comprising less elements mixed together, and being therefore less composite, they would not so easily suffer from adverse influences, and would therefore be less liable to disease than man; their life would also exceed his; for, the more perfect an animal, as a species, the longer its days; thus mankind, whose existence extends beyond that of other animals. For I do not believe in the centenary existence of crows, stags, ravens and the like, of which Pliny tells his customary stories; and although his dreams have been reechoed by others without previous inquiry, it is no less clear that before writing thus, not one has faithfully noted the birth nor the death of those animals: they have been content with taking up the strange fable, as has been the case with the Phoenix, whose longevity is discarded as a story by Tacitus, *Annals*, b. 6. It were therefore to be inferred that the animals we are speaking of would live longer still than man; for, as shall be said below, they would be more noble than he; consequently also, they would be subject to the other bodily affections, and require rest and food, as mentioned, number 50. Now, as rational beings amenable to discipline, they might also continue ignorant, if their minds did not receive the culture of study and instruction, and some amongst them would be more or less versed in science, more or less clever, according as their intelligence had been more or less trained. However, generally speaking, and considering the whole of the species, they would be more learned than men, not from the subtilty of their body, but perhaps because of the greater activity of their mind or the longer space of their life, which would enable them to learn more things than men: such are indeed the motives assigned by S. Austin (*Divin. Demon.* ch. 3 and *Spirit and Soul*, ch. 37), to the presence of the future in Demons. They might indeed suffer from natural agencies; but they could hardly be killed, on account of the speed with which they could escape from danger; it is therefore most unlikely that they could, without the greatest difficulty, be put to death or mutilated by beast or by man, with natural or artificial weapons, so quick would they be at avoiding the impending blow. Yet, they might be killed or mutilated in their sleep, or in a moment of inadvertence, by means of a solid body, such as a sword brandished by a man, or the fall of a heavy stone; for, although subtle, their body would be divisible, just like air which, though vaporous, is yet divided by a sword, a club, or any other solid body. Their spirit, however, would be indivisible, and like the human soul, entire in the whole and in each and every part of the body. Consequently, the division of their body by another body, as aforesaid, might occasion mutilation and even death, for the spirit, itself indivisible, could not animate both parts of a divided body. True, just as the parts of air, separated by the

19

agency of a body, unite again as soon as that body is withdrawn, and constitute the same air as before, even so the parts of the body divided, as above-mentioned, might united and be revived by the same spirit. But then, it must be inferred that those animals could not be slain by natural or artificial agencies: and it were more rational to keep to our first position; for, if sharing matter with other creatures, it is natural that they should be liable to suffer through those creatures, according to the common rule, and even unto death.

59. Sixth question: Could their bodies penetrate other bodies, such as walls, wood, metals, glass, etc.? Could many of them abide together on the same material spot, and to what space would their body extend or be restrained?

60. I reply: In all bodies, however compact, there are pores, as is apparent in metals where, more than in other bodies, it would seem there should be none; through a perfect microscope the pores of metal are discerned, with their different shapes. Now, those animals might, through the pores, creep into, and thus penetrate any other bodies, although such pores were impervious to other liquors or material spirits, of wine, ammoniacal salt, or the like, because their bodies would be much more subtle than those liquors. However, notwithstanding many Angels may abide together on the same material spot, and even confine themselves in a lesser and lesser space, though not infinitely, as is shown by Scott, yet it were rash to ascribe the same power to those animals; for, their bodies are determined in substance and impervious to each other; and if two glorious bodies cannot abide together on the same spot, though a glorious and a non-glorious one may do so, according to some Doctors, much less would it be possible for the bodies of those animals, which are indeed subtle, yet do not attain to the subtility of the glorious body. As regards their power of extension or compression, we may instance the case of air, which, rarefied and condensed, occupies more or less room, and may even, by artificial means, be compressed into a narrower space than would be naturally due to its volume; as is seen with those larges balls which, for amusement, one inflates by means of a blow-pipe or tube: air, being forced into them and compressed, is held in larger quantity than is warranted by the capacity of the ball. Similarly the bodies of the animals we are speaking of might, by their natural virtue, extend to a larger space, not exceeding however their own substance; they might also contract, but not beyond the determined space due to that same substance. And, considering that of their number, as with men, some would be tall and some short, it were proper that the tall should be able to extend more than the short, and the short to contract more than the tall.

61. Seventh question: Would those animals be born in original sin, and have been redeemed by the Lord Christ? Would the grace have been conferred upon them and through what sacraments? Under what law would they live, and would they be capable of beatitude and damnation?

62. I reply: It is an article of belief that Christ has merited grace and glory for all rational creatures without exception. It is also an article of belief that glory is not conferred on a rational creature until such has been previously endowed with

grace, which is the disposition to glory. According to a like article, glory is conferred but by merits. Now, those merits are grounded on the perfect observance of the commands of God, which is accomplished through grace. The above questions are thus solved. Whether those creatures did or did not sin originally is uncertain. It is clear, however, that if their first Parent had sinned as Adam sinned, his descent would be born in original sin, as men are born. And, as God never leaves a rational creature without a remedy, so long as it treads the way, if those creatures were infected with original or with actual sin, God would have provided them with a remedy; but whether it is the case, and of what kind is the remedy, is a secret between God and them. Surely, if they had sacraments identical with or different from those in use in the human Church militant, for the institution and efficacy thereof they would be indebted to the merits of Jesus-Christ, the Redeemer and universal Atoner of all rational creatures. It would likewise be highly proper, nay necessary, that they should live under some law given them by God, and through the observance of which they might merit beatitude; but what would be that law, whether merely natural or written, Mosaic or Evangelical, or different from all these and specially instituted by God, that we are ignorant of. Whatever it might be though, there would follow no objection exclusive of the possible existence of such creatures.

63. The only argument, and that a rather lame one, which long meditations has suggested to me against the possibility of such creatures, is that, if they really existed in the World, we should find them mentioned somewhere by Philosophers, Holy Scripture, Ecclesiastical Tradition, or the Holy Fathers: such not being the case, their utter impossibility should be inferred.

64. But that argument which, in fact, calls in question their existence rather than their possibility, is easily disposed of by our premises, Nrs 41 and 42; for no argument can stand in virtue of a negative authority. Besides, it is not correct to assert that neither the Philosophers, nor the Scriptures, nor the Fathers have handed down any notion of them. Plato, as is reported by Apluleius (*The Demon of Socrates*) and Plutarch (*Isis and Osiris*), declared that Demons were beings of the animal kind, passive souls, rational intelligences, aerial bodies, everlasting; and he gave them the name of *Demons*, which of itself is nowise offensive, since it means *replete with wisdom*; so that, when authors allude to the Devil (or Evil Angel), they do not merely call him Demon, but *Cacodemon*, and say likewise *Eudemon*, when speaking of a good Angel. Those creatures are also mentioned in Scripture and by the Fathers, as shall be said hereafter.

65. Now that we have proved that those creatures are possible, let us go a step further, and show that they exist. Taking for granted the truth of the recitals concerning the intercourse of Incubi and Succubi with men and beasts, recitals so numerous that it would look like impudence to deny the fact, as is said by St Austin, whose testimony is given above (Nr 10), I argue: Where the peculiar passion of the sense is found, there also, of necessity, is the sense itself; for, according to the principles of philosophy, the peculiar passion flows from nature, that is to say: that,

where the acts and operations of the sense are found, there also is the sense, the operations and acts being but its external form. Now, those Incubi and Succubi present acts, operations, peculiar passions, which spring from the senses; they are therefore endowed with senses. But senses cannot exist without concomitant composite organs, without a combination of soul and body. Incubi and Succubi have therefore body and soul, and, consequentially, are animals; but their acts and operations are also those of a rational soul; their soul is therefore rational; and thus, from first to last, they are rational animals.

66. Our minor is easy of demonstration in each of its parts. And indeed, the appetitive passion of coition is a sensual passion; the grief, sadness, wrath, rage, occasioned by the denial of coition, are sensual passions, as is seen with all animals; generation through coition is evidently a sensual operation. Now, all that happens with Incubi, as has been shown above: they incite women, sometimes even men; if denied, they sadden and storm, like lovers: *amentes, amentes*; they perfectly practice coition, and sometimes beget. It must therefore be inferred that they have senses, and consequently a body; consequently also, that they are perfect animals. More than that: with closed doors and windows they enter wherever they please: their body is therefore slender; they foreknow and foretell the future, compose and divide, all which operations are proper to a rational soul; they therefore possess a rational soul and are, in sooth, rational animals.

Doctors generally retort that it is the Evil Spirit that perpetrates those impure acts, simulates passions, love, grief at the denial of coition, in order to entice souls to sin and to undo them; and that, if he copulates and begets, it is with assumed sperm and body, as aforesaid (Nr 24).

67. But then, there are Incubi that have to do with horses, mares and other beasts, and, as shown by every day experience, illtreat them if rebel to coition; yet, in those cases, it can no longer be adduced that the Demon simulates the appetite for coition in order to bring about the ruin of souls, since those of beasts are not capable of everlasting damnation. Besides, love and wrath with them are productive of quite opposite effects. For, if the loved woman or beast humours them, those Incubi behave very well; on the contrary, they use them most savagely when irritated and enraged by a denial of coition: this is amply proved by daily experience: those Incubi therefore have truly sexual passions. Besides, the Evil Spirits, the incorporeal Demons which have to do with Sorceresses and Witches, constrain them to Demon-Worship, to the abjuration of the Orthodox Faith, to the commission of enchantments and foul crimes, as preliminary conditions to the infamous intercourse, as has been above-stated (Nr 11); now, Incubi pretend to nothing of the kind: they are therefore no Evil Spirits. Lastly, as written by Guaccius, at the mere utterance of the name of Jesus or Mary, at the sign of the Cross, the approach of Holy Relics or consecrated objects, at exorcisms, adjurations or priestly injunctions, the Evil Demon either shudders and takes to flight, or is agitated and howls, as is daily seen with energumens and is shown by numerous narratives of Guaccius concerning the nightly revels of Witches, where, at a sign of the Cross or

the name of Jesus said by one of the assistants, Devils and Witches all vanish to-gether. Incubi, on the contrary, stand all those ordeals without taking to flight or showing the least fear; sometimes even they laugh at exorcisms, strike the Exor-cists themselves, and rend the sacred vestments. Now, if the evil Demon, subdued by our Lord Jesus-Christ, are stricken with fear by his name, the Cross and the holy things; if, on the other hand, the good Angels rejoice at those same things, without however inciting men to sin nor to give offense to God, whilst the Incubi, without having any dread of the holy things, provoke to sin, it is clear that they are neither evil Demons nor good Angels; but it is clear also that they are not men, though endowed with reason. What then should they be? Supposing them to have reached the goal, and to be pure spirits, they would be damned or blessed, for correct The-ology does not admit of pure spirits on the way to salvation. If damned, they would revere the name and the Cross of Christ; if blessed, they would not incite men to sin; they would therefore be different from pure spirits, and thus, have a body and be on the way to salvation.

68. Besides, a material agent cannot act but on an equally material passive. It is indeed a trite philosophical axiom, that agent and patient much have a common subject: pure matter cannot act on any purely spiritual thing. Now, there are natural agents which act on those Incubi Demons: these are therefore material or corpo-real. Our minor is proved by the testimony of Dioscorides, Pliny, Aristoteles and Apuleius, quoted by Guaccius, *Compi. Malef.* b. 3, ch. 13, fol. 316; it is confirmed by our knowledge of numerous herbs, stones and animal substances which have the virtue of driving away Demons, such as rue, St-John's wort, verbena, germander, palma Christi, centaury, diamonds, coral, jet, jasper, the skin of the head of a wolf or an ass, women's catamenia, and a hundred others: wherefore it is written: *For such as are assaulted by the Demon it is lawful to have stones or herbs, but without recourse to incantations.* It follows that, by their own native virtue, stones or herbs can bridle the Demon: else the above mentioned Canon would not permit their use, but would on the contrary forbid it as superstitious. We have a striking instance thereof in Holy Scripture, where the Angel Raphael says to Tobit, ch. 6, v. 8, speaking of the fish which he had drawn from the Tigris: *"If thou puttest on coals a particle of its liver, the smoke thereof will drive away all kinds of Demons."* Experience demonstrated the truth of those words; for, no sooner was the liver of the fish set on fire, than the Incubus who was in love with Sarah put to flight.

69. To this Theologians usually retort that such natural agents merely initiate the ejection of the Demon, and that the completive effect is due to the supernatu-ral force of God or of the Angel; so that the supernatural force is the primary, di-rect and principal cause, the natural force being but secondary, indirect and subor-dinate. Thus, in order to explain how the liver of the fish burnt by Tobit drove away the Demon, Vallesius asserts that the smoke thereof had been endowed by God with the supernatural power of expelling the Incubus, in the same manner as the material fire of Hell has the virtue of tormenting Demons and the souls of the Damned. Others, such as Lyranus and Cornelius, profess that the smoke of the

heart of the fish initiated the ejection of the Demon by native virtue, but completed in by angelical and heavenly virtue: by native virtue, insomuch that it opposed a contrary action to that of the Demon; for the Evil Spirit applies native causes and humours, the native qualities of which are combated by the contrary qualities of natural things known to be capable of driving away Demons; that opinion is shared by all those who treat of the art of exorcisms.

70. But that explanation, however plausible the facts upon which it rests, can at most be received as regards the Evil Spirits which possess bodies or, through malefice, infect them with diseases or other infirmities; it does not at all meet the case of Incubi. For, these neither possess bodies nor infect them with disease; they, at most, molest them by blows and ill-treatment. If they cause the mares to grow lean because of their not yielding to coition, it is merely by taking away their provender, in consequence of which they fall off and finally die. To that purpose the Incubus need not use a natural agent, as the Evil Spirit does when imparting a disease: it is enough that it should exert its own native organic force. Likewise, when the evil Spirit possesses bodies and infects them with diseases, it is most frequently through signs agreed upon with himself, and arranged by a witch or a wizard, which signs are usually natural objects, imbued with their own noxious virtue, and of course opposed by other equally natural objects endowed with a contrary virtue. But not so the Incubus: it is of his own accord, and without the cooperation of either witch or wizard, that he inflicts his molestations. Besides, the natural things which put the Incubi to flight exert their virtue and bring about a results without the intervention of any exorcism or blessing; it cannot therefore be said that the ejection of the Incubus is initiated by natural, and completed by divine virtue, since there is in this case no particular invocation of the divine name, but the mere effect of a natural object, in which God cooperates only as the universal agent, the author of nature, the first of efficient causes.

71. To illustrate this subject, I give two stories, the first of which I have from a Confessor of Nuns, a man of weight, and most worthy of credit; the second I was eye-witness to. In a certain monastery of holy Nuns there lived, as a boarder, a young maiden of noble birth, who was tempted by an Incubus that appeared to her by day and by night, and with the most earnest entreaties, the manners of a most passionate lover, incessantly incited her to sin; but she, supported by the grace of God and the frequent use of the sacraments, stoutly resisted the temptation. But, all her devotions, fasts and vows notwithstanding, despite the exorcisms, the blessings, the injunctions showered by exorcists on the Incubus that he should desist from molesting her; in spite of the crowd of relics and other holy objects collected in the maiden's room, of the lighted candles kept burning there all night, the Incubus none the less persisted in appearing to her as usual, in the shape of a very handsome young man. At last, among other learned men, whose advice had been taken on the subject, was a very erudite Theologian who, observing that the maiden was of a thoroughly phlegmatic temperament, surmised that that Incubus was an aqueous Demon (there are in fact, as is testified by Guaccius, igneous, aerial,

phlegmatic, earthly, subterranean demons who avoid the light of day), and prescribed an uninterrupted fumigation in the room. A new vessel, made of glass-like
earth, was accordingly brought in, and filled with sweet cane, cubeb seed, roots of
both artistolochies, great and small cardamon, ginger, long-pepper, caryophylleae,
cinnamon, cloves, mace, nutmegs, calamite storax, benzoin, aloes-wood and roots,
one ounce of triasandalis, and three pounds of half brandy and water; the vessel
was then set on hot ashes in order to force up the fumigating vapour, and the cell
was kept closed. As soon as the fumigation was done, the Incubus came, but never
dared enter the cell; only, if the maiden left it for a walk in the garden or the clois-
ter, he appeared to her, though invisible to others and throwing his arms round her
neck, stole or rather snatched kisses from her, to her intense disgust. At last, after a
new consultation, the Theologian prescribed that she should carry about her person pills made of the most exquisite perfumes, such as musk, amber, chive, Peru-
vian balsam, and others. Thus provided, she went for a walk in the garden, where
the Incubus suddenly appeared to her with a threatening face, and in a rage. He did
not approach her, however, but, after biting his finger as if meditating revenge,
disappeared and was never more seen by her.

72. Here is the other story. In the great Carthusian Friary of Pavia there lived
a Deacon, Austin by name, who was subjected by a certain Demon to excessive,
unheard of and scarcely credible vexations; although many exorcists had made re-
peated endeavors to secure his riddance, all spiritual remedies had proved unavail-
ing. I was consulted by the Vicar of the convent, who had the cure of the poor
clerk. Seeing the inefficacy of all customary exorcisms, and remembering the
above-related instance, I advised a fumigation like unto the one that has been de-
tailed, and prescribed that the Deacon should carry about his person fragrant pills
of the same kind; moreover, as he was in the habit of using tobacco, and was very
fond of brandy, I advised tobacco and brandy perfumed with musk. The Demon
appeared to him by day and by night, under various shapes, as a skeleton, a pig, an
ass, and Angel, a bird; with the figure of one or other of the Friars, once even with
that of his own Abbot or Prior, exhorting him to keep his conscience clean, to
trust in God, to confess frequently; he persuaded him to let him near his sacramental confession, recited with him the psalms *Exsurgat Deus* and *Qui habitat*, and the
Gospel according to St John: and when they came to the words *Verbum caro factum
est*, he bent his knee, and taking hold of a stole which was in the cell, and of the
Holy-water sprinkle, he blessed the cell and the bed, and, as if he had really been
the Prior, enjoined on the Demon not to venture in future to molest his subordi-
nate; he then disappeared, thus betraying what he was, for otherwise the young
deacon had taken him for his Prior. Now, notwithstanding the fumigations and
perfumes I had prescribed, the Demon did not desist from his wonted apparitions;
more than that, assuming the features of his victim, he went to the Vicar's room,
and asked for some tobacco and brandy perfumed with musk, of which, said he, he
was extremely fond. Having received both, he disappeared in the twinkling of an
eye, thus showing the Vicar that he had been played with by the Demon; and this

was amply confirmed by the Deacon, who affirmed upon his oath that he had not gone that day to the Vicar's cell. All that having been related to me, I inferred that, far from being aqueous like the Incubus who was in love with the maiden above spoken of, this Demon was igneous, or, at the very least, aerial, since he delighted in hot substances such as vapours, perfumes, tobacco and brandy. Force was added to my surmises by the temperament of the young deacon, which was choleric and sanguine, choler predominating however; for, those Demons never approach but those whose temperament tallies with their own: another confirmation of my sentiment regarding their corporeity. I therefore advised the Vicar to let his penitent take herbs that are cold by nature, such as water-lily, liver-wort, spurge, mandrake, house-leek, plantain, henbane, and others similar, make two little bundles of them and hang them up, one at his window, the other at the door of his cell, taking care to strow some also on the floor and on the bed. Marvellous to say! The Demon appeared again, but remained outside the room., which he would not enter; and, on the Deacon inquiring of him his motives for such unwonted reserve, he burst out into invectives against me for giving such advice, disappeared, and never came again.

73. The two stories I have related make it clear that, by their native virtue alone, perfumes and herbs drove away Demons without the intervention of any supernatural force; Incubi are therefore subject to material conditions, and it must be inferred that they participate of the matter of the natural objects which have the power of putting them to flight, and consequently they have a body; that is what was to be shown.

74. But, the better to establish our conclusion, it behooves to impugn the mistake into which have fallen the Doctors above-quoted, such as Vallesius and Cornelius a Lapide, when they say that Sarah was rid from the Incubus by the virtue of the Angel Raphael, and not by that of the callionymous fish caught by Tobit on the banks of the Tigris. Indeed, saving the reverence due to such great doctors, such a construction manifestly clashes with the clear meaning of the Text, from which it is never justifiable to deviate, so long as it does not lead to absurd consequences. Here are the words spoken by the Angel to Tobias: "*If thou puttest on coals a particle of its heart, the smoke thereof will expel all kinds of Demons, whether from man or woman, so that they shall never return, and its gall is good for anointing eyes that have whiteness, and healing them*" (Tobit, c. 6, v. 8 and 9). Pray notice that the Angel's assertion respecting the virtue of the heart or liver and gall of that fish is absolute, universal; for, he does not say: "*If thou puttest on coals particles of its heart, thou wilt put to flight all kinds of Demons, and if thou anointest with its gall eyes that have a whiteness, they shall be healed.*" If he had thus spoken, I could agree with the construction that Raphael had brought about, by his own supernatural virtue, the effects which the mere application of the smoke and the gall might not have sufficed to produce: but he does not speak thus, and, on the contrary, says absolutely, that such is the virtue of the smoke and the gall.

75. It may be asked whether the Angel spoke the precise truth regarding the virtue of those things, or whether he might have lied; and likewise, whether the whiteness was withdrawn from the eyes of the elder Tobit by the native force of the gall of the fish, or by the supernatural virtue of the Angel Raphael? To say that the Angel could have lied would be an heretical blasphemy; he therefore spoke the precise truth; but it would no longer be so if all kinds of Demons were not expelled by the smoke of the liver of the fish, unless aided by the supernatural force of the Angel, and especially, if such aid was the principal cause of the effect produced, as the Doctors assert in the present case. It would doubtless be a lie if a physician should say: such an herb radically cures pleurisy or epilepsy, and if it should only being the cure, the completion of which required the addition of another herb to the one first used; in the same manner, Raphael would have lied when averring that the smoke of the liver expelled all kinds of demons, so that they should not return, if that result had been only begun by the smoke, and its completion had been principally due to the virtue of the Angel. Besides, that flight of the demon was either to take place universally and by any one whomsoever putting the liver of the fish on the coals, or else it was only to occur in that particular case, the younger Tobit putting the liver on. In the first hypothesis, any person making that smoke by burning the liver should be assisted by an Angel, who, through his supernatural virtue should expel the Demons miraculously and regularly at the same time; which is absurd; for, either words have no meaning, or a natural fact cannot be regularly followed by a miracle; and, if the Demon was not put to flight without the assistance of the Angel, Raphael would have lied when ascribing that virtue to the liver. If, on the contrary, that effect was only to be brought about in that particular case, Raphael would again have lied when assigning to that fish, universally and absolutely, the virtue of expelling the Demon: now, to say that the Angel lied is not possible.

76. The whiteness was withdrawn from the eyes of the elder Tobit, and his blindness healed, through the native virtue of the gall of the same fish, as Doctors aver. In fact, that the gall of the callionymous fish, which the Italians call *bocca in capo*, and of which Tobias made use, is a highly renowned remedy for removing the whiteness from the eyes, all are agreed, Dioscorides, Galen, Pliny, Aclanius, Vallesius, etc. The Greek Text of *Tobit*, c. 11, v. 13, says: "*He poured the gall on his father's eyes, saying: Have confidence, father; but, there being erosion, the old man rubbed his eyes, and the scaled of the whiteness came out at the corners.*" Now, since, according to the same text, the Angel had disclosed to Tobias the virtue of the liver and gall of the fish, and since, through its native virtue, the gall cured the elder Tobit's blindness, it must be inferred that it was likewise through its native force that the smoke of the liver put the Incubus to flight; which inference is conclusively confirmed by the Greek text, which, *Tobit*, c. 8, v. 2, instead of the reading in the Vulgate: "*He laid a part of the liver on burning coals,*" says explicitly: *He took the ashes of the perfumes, and put the heart and the liver of the fish thereupon, and made a smoke therewith; the which smell when the evil*

*spirit had smelled, he fled.*" The Hebrew text says: "*Asmodeus smelled the smell, and fled.*" From all those texts it appears that the Demon took to flight on smelling a smoke which was prejudicial and hurtful to himself, and nowise from the supernatural virtue of the Angel. If, in ridding Sarah from the assaults of the Incubus Asmodeus, the operation of the smoke of the liver was followed by the intervention of Raphael, it was in order to bind the Demon in the wilderness of High-Egypt, as related, *Tobit*, c. 8, v. 3; for, at such a distance, the smoke of the liver could neither operate on the Demon, nor bind him. And here we have the means of reconciling our opinion with that of the above-mentioned Doctors, who ascribe to Raphael's power Sarah's complete riddance from the Demon: for, I say with them, that the cure of Sarah was completed by the binding of the Demon in the wilderness, the deed of the Angel; which I concede; but I maintain that the deliverance properly called, that is to say, the ejection from Sarah's bed-room, was the direct effect of the virtue of the liver of the fish.

77. A third principal proof of our conclusion regarding the existence of those animals, in other words, respecting the corporeity of Incubi, is adduced by the testimony of St Hieronymus, in his *Life of St Paul, the first Hermit*. St Anthony, says he, set on a journey to visit St Paul. After travelling several days, he met a Centaur, of whom he inquired the hermit's abode; whereupon the Centaur, growling some uncouth and scarcely intelligible answer, shew the way with his out-stretched hand, and fled with the utmost speed into a wood. The Holy Abbot kept on his way, and, in a dale, met a little man, almost a dwarf, with crooked hands, horned brow, and his lower extremities ending with goat's feet. At the sight of him, St Anthony stood still, and fearing the arts of the Devil, comforted himself with a sing of the Cross. But, far from running away, or even seeming frightened at it, the little fellow respectfully approached the old man, and tendered him, as a peace offering, dates for his journey. The blessed St Anthony having then inquired who he was: "*I am a mortal,*" replied he, "*and one of the inhabitants of the Wilderness, whom Gentility, under its varied delusions, worships under the names of Fauns, Satyrs and Incubi; I am on a mission from my flock: we request thee to pray for us unto the common God, whom we know to have come for the salvation of the world, and whose praises are sounded all over the earth.*" Rejoicing at the glory of Christ, St Anthony, turning his face towards Alexandria, and striking the ground with his staff, cried out: "*Woe be unto thee, thou harlot City, who worshipest animals as Gods!*" Such is the narrative of St Hieronymus, who expatiates at length on the fact, explaining its import in a long discourse.

78. It were indeed rash to doubt the truth of the above recital, constantly referred to by the greatest of the Doctors of the Holy Church, St Hieronymus, whose authority no Catholic will ever deny. Let us therefore investigate the circumstances thereof which most clearly confirm our opinion.

79. Firstly, we must observe that if ever a Saint was assailed by the arts of the Demon, saw through his infernal devices, and carried off victories and trophies from the contest, that Saint was St Anthony, as is shown by his life written by St Athanasius. Now, since in that little man St Anthony did not recognize a devil but

an animal, saying: "*Woe be unto thee, thou harlot City, who worshipest animals as Gods!*", it is clear that it was no devil or pure spirit ejected from heaven and damned, but some kind of animal. Still more: St Anthony, when instructing his friars and cautioning them against the assaults of the Demon, said to them, as related in the Roman Breviary (*Festival of St Anthony, Abbot*, b. I): "*Believe me, my brethren, Satan dreads the vigils of pious men, their prayers, fasts, voluntary poverty, compassion and humility; but, above all, he dreads their burning love of our Lord Christ, at the mere sign of whose most Holy Cross he flies disabled.*" As the little man, against whom St Anthony guarded himself with a sign of the Cross, neither took fright now fled, but approached the Saint confidently and humbly, offering him some dates, it is a sure sign that he was no Devil.

80. Secondly, we must observe that the little man said: "*I also am a mortal,*" whence it follows that he was an animal subject to death, and consequently called into being through generation; for, an immaterial spirit is immortal, because simple, and consequently is not called into being through generation from preexistent matter, but through creation, and, consequently also, cannot lose it through the corruption called death; its existence can only come to an end though annihilation. Therefore, when saying he was mortal, he professed himself an animal.

81. Thirdly, we must observe that he said he knew that the common God had suffered in human flesh. Those words show him to have been a rational animal, for brutes know nothing but what is sensible and present, and can therefore have no knowledge of God. If that little man said he and his fellows were aware of God having suffered in human flesh, it shows that, by means of some revelation, he had acquired the notion of God, as we have ourselves the revealed faith. That God assumed human flesh and suffered in it, is the essence of the two principal articles of our Faith: the existence of God one and threefold, His Incarnation, Passion and Resurrection. All that shows, as I said, that it was a rational animal, capable of the knowledge of God through revelation, like ourselves, and endowed with a rational, and consequently, immortal soul.

82. Fourthly, we must observe that, in the name of his whole flock whose delegate he professed to be, he besought St Anthony to pray for them to the common God. Wherefrom I infer that that little man was capable of beatitude and damnation, and that he was not *in termino* but *in via*; for, from his being, as has been shown above, rational and consequently endowed with an immortal soul, it flows that he was capable of beatitude and damnation, the proper share of every rational Creature, Angel or man. I likewise infer that he was on the way, *in via*, that is, capable of merit and demerit; for, if he had been at the goal, *in termino*, he would have been either blessed or damned. Now, he could be neither the one nor the other; for, St Anthony's prayers, to which he commended himself, could have been of no assistance to him, if finally damned, and, if blessed, he stood in no need of them. Since he commended himself to this prayers, it shows they could be of avail to him, and, consequently, that he was on the way to salvation, *in statu viae et meriti*.

83. Fifthly, we must observe that the little man professed to be delegated by others of his kind, when saying: *"I am on a mission from my flock,"* words from which many inferences may be deduced. One is, that the little man was not alone of his kind, an exceptional and solitary monster, but that there were many of the same species, since congregating they made up a flock, and that he came in the name of all; which could not have been, had not the will of many centered in him. Another is, that those animals lead a social life, since one of them was sent in the name of many. Another again is, that, although living in the Wilderness, it is not assigned to them as a permanent abode; for St Anthony having never previously been in that desert, which was far distant from his hermitage, they could not have known who he was nor what his degree of sanctity; it was therefore necessary that they should have become acquainted with him elsewhere, and, consequently, that they should have travelled beyond that wilderness.

84. Lastly, we must observe that the little man said he was one of those whom *the Gentiles, blinded by error, call Fauns, Satyrs and Incubi*: and by these words is shown the truth of our principal proposition: that Incubi are rational animals, capable of beatitude and damnation.

85. The apparition of such little men is of frequent occurrence in metallic mines, as is written by Gregorius Agricola in his book *De Animal. subterran.* They appear to the miners, clothed like themselves, play and caper together, laugh and titter, and throw little stones at them for the sake of amusement: a sign, says the above-named Author, of excellent success, and of the finding of some branch or body of a mineral tree.

86. Peter Thyraeus, of Neuss, in his book *De Terrification. nocturne.*, denies the existence of such little men, and supports his denial upon the following truly puerile arguments: given such little men, says he, where do they live, how and where do they dwell? How do they keep up their kind, through generation or otherwise? Are they born, do they die, with what food do they sustain themselves? Are they capable of beatitude and damnation, and by what means do they procure their salvation? Such are the arguments upon which Thyraeus relies for denying that existence.

87. But it really shows little judgment in a man, to deny that which has been written by grave and credible Authors, and confirmed by every day experience. Thyraeus's arguments are worthless and have been already refuted, Nrs 45 and following. The only question which remains to be answered is this: where do those little men, or Incubi, dwell? To that I reply: as has been shown above (Nr 71), according to Guaccius, some are earthly, some aqueous, some aerial, some igneous, that is to say, that their bodies are made of the most subtle part of one of the elements, or, if of the combination of many elements, that yet there is one which predominates, either water or air, according to their nature. Their dwellings will consequently be found in that element which is prevalent in their bodies: igneous Incubi, for instance, will only stay forcibly, may be will not stay at all, in water or marshes, which are adverse to them; and aqueous Incubi will not be able to rise into the upper part of either, the subtlety of which region is repugnant to them. We

see the like happen to men who, accustomed to thicker air, cannot reach certain lofty ridges of the Alps where the air is too subtle for their lungs.

88. Many testimonies of Holy Fathers, gathered by Molina, in his *Commentary of St Thomas*, would go to prove the corporeity of Demons but, taking into account the above-quoted decision of the Council of Lateran (Nr 37), concerning the incorporeity of Angels, we must understand that the Holy Fathers had in view those Incubi Demons which are still on the way to salvation, and not those that are damned. However, to make matters short, we merely give the authority of St Austin, that eminent Doctor of the Church, and it would be clearly seen how thoroughly his doctrine harmonizes with ours.

89. St Austin, then, in his *Commentary on Genesis*, book 2, ch. 17, writes as follows concerning Demons: "*They have the knowledge of some truths, partly through the more subtle acumen of their sense, partly through the greater subtilty of their bodies*," and, book 3, ch. I: "*Demons are aerial animals, because they partake of the nature of aerial bodies.*" In his Epistle 115 to Hebridius, he affirms that they are "*aerial or ethereal animals, endowed with very sharp senses.*" In the *City of God*, book 11, ch. 13, he says that "*the worst Demon has an aerial body.*" Book 21, ch. 10, he writes: "*The bodies of certain Demons, as has been believed by some learned men, are even made of the thick and damp air which we breathe.*" Book 15, ch. 23: "*He dares not define whether Angels, with an aerial body, could feel the lust which would incite them to communicated with women.*" In his commentary on Psalm 85, he says that "*the bodies of the blessed will, after resurrection, be like unto the bodies of Angels;*" Psalm 14, he observes that "*the body of Angels is inferior to the soul.*" And, in his book *De Divinit. Daemonum*, he every-where, and especially ch. 23, teaches that "*Demons have subtle bodies.*"

90. Our doctrine can also be confirmed by the testimony of the Holy Scriptures, which, however diversely construed by commentators, are yet capable of adaptation to our proposition. First, Psalm 77, v. 24 and 25, it is said: "*The Lord had given them of the bread of heaven; man did eat angels' food.*" David here alludes to Manna, which fed the People of Israel during the whole time that they wandered in the wilderness. It will be asked in what sense it can be said of Manna that it is the *Bread of Angels*. I am aware that most Doctors construe this passage in a mystical sense, saying that Manna figures the Holy Eucharist, which is styled the *bread of Angels*, because Angels enjoy the sight of God who, by concomitance, is found in the Eucharist.

91. A most proper construction assuredly, and which is adopted by the Church in the office of the *Most Holy Body of Jesus-Christ*; but it is in a spiritual sense. Now, what I want, is the literal sense; for, in that Psalm, David does not speak, as a prophet, of things to be, as he does in other places where a literal sense is not easily to be gathered; he speaks here as a historian, of things gone by. That Psalm, as is evident to whoever reads it, is a pure anacephalaeosis, or summing up of all the benefits conferred by God on the Hebrew People from the exodus from Egypt to the days of David, and the Manna of the Wilderness is spoken of in it; how, and in what sense is it styled the Bread of Angels? That is the question.

31

92. I am aware that others look upon the Bread of Angels as bread prepared by Angels, or sent down from Heaven by the ministry of Angels. But Cardinal Hugo explains that qualification by saying that that food partly produced the same effect upon the Jews, which the food of Angels produces upon the latter. Angels, in fact, are not liable to any infirmity; on the other hand Hebrew commentators, and Josephus himself, assert that whilst in the Wilderness, living upon Manna, the Jews neither grew old, nor sickened, nor tired; so that Manna was like unto the bread that Angels feed upon, who know neither old age, nor sickness, nor fatigue.

93. These interpretations should indeed be received with the respect due to the authority of such eminent Doctors. There is however one difficulty in this: that, by the ministry of Angels, the pillars of the cloud and fire, the quails, and the water from the rock were provided for the Hebrews, no less than the Manna; and yet they were not styled the pillar, the water or the beverage of Angels. Why therefore should Manna be called *Bread of Angels*, because provided by their ministry, when the qualification *Beverage of Angels* is not given to the water drawn from the rock likewise by their ministry? Besides, in Holy Scripture, when it is said of bread that it is the *bread of somebody*, it is always the *bread of him* who feeds on it, not of him who provides or makes it. Of this there are numberless instances: thus, *Exodus*, ch. 23, v. 25: "*That I may bless thy bread and thy water;*" *Kings*, book 2, ch. 12, v. 3: "*Eating of his bread;*" *Tobit*, ch. 4, v. 17: "*Give of thy bread to the hungry,*" and v. 18: "*Pour out thy bread on the burial of the Just;*" *Ecclesiasticus*, ch. 11, v. 1: "*Scatter thy bread over the flowing waters;*" *Isaiah*, ch. 58, v. 7: "*Deal thy bread to the hungry;*" *Jeremiah*, ch. 11, v. 19: "*Let us put wood into his bread;*" *Matthew*, ch. 15, v. 26: "*It is not meet to take the children's bread;*" *Luke*, ch. 11, v. 3: "*Our daily bread.*" All those passages clearly show that, in Scripture, the bread of somebody is the bread of him who feeds upon it, not of him who makes, brings or provides it. In the passage of the Psalm we have quoted, *Bread of Angels* may therefore easily be taken to mean the food of Angels, not incorporeal indeed, since these required no material food, but corporeal, that is to say of those rational animals we have discoursed of, who live in the air, and, from the subtlety of their bodies and their rationality, approximate so closely to immaterial Angels as to fall under the same denomination.

94. I deduce that, being animals, consequently reproducible through generation and liable to corruption, they require food for the restoration of their corporeal substance wasted by effluvia: for the life of every sensible being consists in nothing else but the motion of the corporeal elements which flow and ebb, are acquired, lost and recruited by means of substances spirituous, yet material, assimilated by the living thing, either through the inhalation of air, or by the fermentation of food which spiritualizes its substance, as shown by the most learned Ettmuller (*Instit. Medic. Physiolog.*, ch. 2).

95. But, their body being subtle, equally subtle and delicate must be its food. And, just as perfumes and other vaporous and volatile substances, when adverse to their nature, offend and put them to flight, as testified by what we related above (Nrs 71 and 72), in the like manner, when agreeable, they delight in and feed upon

them. Now, as is written by Cornelius, "*Manna is nothing but an emanation of water and earth, refined and baked by the heat of the sun, and then coagulated and condensed by the cold of the following night;*" of course, I am speaking of the Manna sent down from Heaven, and which differs all in all from nostrate or medicinal manna: the latter, in fact, according to Ettmuller (*Dilucid. Physiol.*, ch. 1), "*is merely the juice or transudation of certain trees which, during the night, gets mixed up with dew, and, the next morning, coagulates and thickens in the heat of the sun.*" The manna of the Hebrews, on the contrary, derived from other principles, far from coagulating, liquefied in the heat of the sun, as is shown by Scripture, *Exodus*, ch. 16, v. 22. The manna of the Hebrews was therefore undoubtedly of a most subtle substance, consisting as it did of emanations of earth and water, and being dissolved by the sun and made to disappear: consequently, it may very well have been the food of the animals we are speaking of, and thus have been truly called by David *Bread of Angels*.

96. We have another authority in the Gospel according to St John, ch. 10, v. 16, where it is said: "*And other sheep I have, which are not of this fold: them also I must bring, and they shall hear my voice, and there shall be one fold and one shepherd.*" If we inquire what are those sheep which are not of that fold, and what the fold of which the Lord Christ speaketh, we are answered by all Commentators that the only fold on Christ is the Church to which the preaching of the Gospel was to bring the Gentiles, sheep of another fold than that of the Hebrews. They are, in fact, of opinion that the fold of Christ was the Synagogue, because David had said, Psalm 95, v. 7: "*We are the people of his pasture, and the sheep of his hand,*" and also because Abraham and David had been promised that the Messiah should be born of their race, because he was expected by the Hebrew people, foretold by the Prophets who were Hebrews, and that his advent, his acts, his passion, death and resurrection were prefigured in the sacrifices, worship and ceremonials of the Hebrew law.

97. But, saving always the reverence due to the Holy Father and other Doctors, that explanation does not seem quite satisfactory. For it is an article of belief that the Church of the Faithful has been the only one in existence from the beginning of the world, and will thus endure to the end of time. The head of that Church is Jesus-Christ, the mediator between God and men, by whose contemplation all things were made and created. Indeed, the faith in the divine Trinity, though less explicitly, and the Incarnation of the Word were revealed to the first man, and by him taught his children, who, in their turn, taught them their descendants. And thus, although most men had strayed into idolatry and deserted the true faith, many kept the faith they had received from their fathers, and observing the law of nature, stayed in the true Church of the Faithful, as is noticed by Cardinal Tolet in reference to Job, who was a saint among idolatrous Gentiles. And, although God had conferred especial favours upon the Hebrew people, prescribed for them peculiar laws and ceremonials, and separated them from the Gentiles, yet those laws were not obligatory on the Gentiles, and the faithful Hebrews did not constitute a Church different from that of the Gentiles who professed their faith in one God and the coming of the Messiah.

98. And thus it came to pass that even among the Gentiles there were some who prophesied the advent of Christ and the other dogmas of the Christian faith, to wit *Balaam, Mercurius Trismegistus, Hydaspes,* and the *Sibyls* mentioned by Lactantius, book 1, ch. 6, as written by Baronius, *Apparat. Annal.,* no 18. That the Messiah was expected by the Gentiles is shown by many passages of Isiah, and plainly testified by the prophecy of Jacob, the Patriarch, thus worded, Genesis, ch. 49, v. 10: *"The scepter shall not depart from Judah, nor a law-giver from between his feet, until Shiloh (he who is to be sent) come, and unto him shall the gathering of the people be."* Likewise in the prophecy of Haggai, ch. 2, v. 8: *"I will shake all Nations, and the desire of all Nations shall come";* which passage is thus commented by Cornelius a Lapide: *"The Gentiles before the advent of Christ, who believed in God and observed the law of nature, expected and desired Christ equally with the Jews."* Christ himself disclosed and manifested himself to the Gentiles as well as to the Jews; for, at the same time as the Angel apprized the shepherds of his nativity, by means of the miraculous star he called the Magi to worship him, who, being Gentiles, were the first among the Nations, as the shepherds among the Jews, to acknowledge and worship Christ (*Vide* St Fulgentius, *Sermon 6, upon Epiphany*). In like manner, the advent of Christ was made known by preaching (I am not speaking of the Apostles) to the Gentiles before it was to the Jews. As is written by the Venerable Mother, Sister Maria of Agreda, in her *Life of Jesus-Christ and the Blessed Virgin Mary:* *"When the Blessed Virgin Mary, fleeing with St Joseph, from the persecution of Herod, carried the Infant Jesus into Egypt, she tarried there seven years; and, during that time, the Blessed Virgin herself preached to the Egyptians the faith of the true God and the advent of the Son of God in human flesh."* Besides, the nativity of Christ was attended by numerous prodigies, not only in Judea, but also in Egypt, where the idols tumbled and the oracles were hushed; in Rome, where a spring of oil gushed out, a gold-coloured globe was seen to descend from the skies on earth, three suns appeared, and an extraordinary ring, variegated like a rainbow, encircled the disc of then sun; in Greece, where the oracle of Delphi was struck dumb, and Apollo, asked the reason of his silence by Augustus, who was offering up a sacrifice in his own palace where he had raised an altar to him, answered:

*"A Hebrew child, who sways the Gods, and himself a God,*
*Bids me quit my seat and return to the infernal regions;*
*Depart therefore from our altars, henceforward mute."*

There were many more prodigies warning the Gentiles of the advent of the Son of God: they have been collected from various Authors, by Baronius, and are the be found in his *Apparat. Annal. Eccles.,* and Cornelius, *Commentary upon Haggai.*

99. From all this it is clear that the Gentiles also belonged, like the Jews, to the fold of Christ, that is, to the same Church of the Faithful; it cannot therefore be correctly said that the words of Christ: *"Other sheep I have, which are not of this fold,"* are applicable to the Gentiles, who had, in common with the Hebrews, the faith in

God, the hope, prophecy, expectation, prodigies and preaching of the Messiah.

100. I therefore say that by the words *other sheep* may very well be understood those rational Creatures or animas of whom we have been treating hitherto. They being, as we have said, capable of beatitude and damnation, and Jesus-Christ being the mediator between God and man, as also every rational Creature (for rational creatures attain to beatitude in consideration of the merits of Christ, through the grace he confers upon them, without which beatitude is impossible of attainment), every rational creature must have cherished, at the same time as the faith in one God, the hope of the advent of Christ, and have had the revelation of his nativity in the flesh and of the principles of the law of grace. Those were therefore the sheep which were not *of that human fold,* and which Christ had to bring; the sheep which were to hear His voice, that is, the announcement of His advent and of the evangelical doctrine, either directly through Himself, or through the Apostles; the sheep which, partaking with men of heavenly beatitude, were to realize *one fold and one shepherd.*

101. To this interpretation, which I hold to be in no way improper, force is added by what we related, according to St Hieronymus, of that little man who requested St Anthony to *pray,* for him and his fellows, unto the common God, whom he knew to have suffered in human flesh. For, it implies that they were aware of the advent of the death of Christ, whom, as God, they were anxious to propitiate, since they sought, to that effect, the intercession of St Anthony.

102. Thereto tends also the fact mentioned by Cardinal Baronius (*Appar. Annal.* no 129), after Eusebius and Plutarch, as being one of the prodigies which took place at the time of the death of Christ. He relates that in the reign of the Emperor Tiberius, when Christ suffered, whilst mariners bound from Greece to Italy, were by night, and during a calm, in the vicinity of the Echinade Isles, their ship was brought close to land. All the crew heard a loud voice calling Tramnus, the master of the ship. He having answered to his name, the voice replied: "When near such a march, announce that *the great Pan is dead.*" Which Tramnus having done, there arose suddenly, as from a numberless multitude, groans and shrieks. Doubtless, they were Demons, or corporeal Angels, or rational animals living near the march on account of their aqueous nature, and who, hearing of the death of Christ, described by the name of Great Pan, Burst into tears and bewailing, like some of the Jews who, after witnessing the death of Christ, went home smiting their breasts (*Luke,* ch. 23, v. 48). From all that has been deduced above, it is therefore clear that there are such Demons, succubi and incubi, endowed with senses and subject to the passions thereof, as has been shown; who are born through generation and die through corruption, are capable of beatitude and damnation, more noble than man, by reason of the greater subtilty of their bodies, and who, when having intercourse with man, male or female, fall into the same sin as man when copulating with a beast, which is inferior to him. Also, it not unfrequently occurs that those Demons slay the men, women or mares with whom they have had protracted intercourse;

and the reason is that, being liable to sin whilst on the way to salvation, *in via*, they must likewise be open to repentance; and, in the same manner as a man, who habitually sins with a beast, is enjoined by his confessor to destroy that beast, with a view to suppressing the occasion of relapsing, it may likewise happen that the penitent demon should slay the animal with which it sinned, whether man or beast; nor will death thus occasioned to a man be reckoned a sin to the Demon, any more than death inflicted on a beast is imputed as a sin to man; for, considering the essential difference between a Demon of that kind and man, the man will be the same thing to the Demon as the beast is to man.

103. I am aware that many, perhaps most of my reader, will say of me what the Epicureans and some Stoic Philosophers said of St Paul (*Acts of the Apostles*, ch. 17, v. 18). "*He seemeth to be a setter forth of strange gods,*" and will deride my doctrine. But they will none the less have to answer the foregoing arguments, to show what are those Incubi Demons, commonly called *Goblins*, who dread neither exorcisms, nor the holy things, nor the Cross of Christ, and to explain the various effects and phenomena related when propounding that doctrine.

104. What we have hitherto deduced accordingly solves the question laid down Nrs 30 and 34, to wit: how a woman can be got with child by an Incubus Demon? In fact, it cannot be brought about by sperm assumed from a man, agreeably to the common opinion which we confuted, Nrs 31 and 32; it follows, therefore, that she is directly impregnated by the sperm of the Incubus, which, being an animal and capable of breeding, has sperm of its own. And thus is fully explained the begetting of Giants from the intercourse of the Sons of God with the Daughters of men: for that intercourse gave birth to Giants who, although like unto men, were of higher stature, and, though begotten by Demons, and consequently of great strength, yet equaled them neither in might nor in power. It is the same with mules, which are intermediate, as it were, between the kinds of animals from whose promiscuousness they are sprung, and which excel indeed the most imperfect, but never equal the most perfect: thus, the mule excels the ass, but does not attain the perfection of the mare, which have begotten it.

105. In confirmation of the above inference, we observe that animals sprung from the mixing of different kinds do not breed, but are barren, as is seen with mules. Now we do not read of Giants having been begotten by other Giants, but of their having been born of the Sons of God, that is Incubi, and the Daughters of men: being thus begotten of the Demoniac sperm mixed with the human sperm, and being, as it were, an intermediate species between the Demon and man, they had no generative power.

106. It may be objected that the sperm of Demons, which must, by nature, be most fluid, could not mix with the human sperm, which is thick, and that, consequently, no generation would ensue.

107. I reply that, as has been said above, Nr 32, the generative power lies in the spirit that comes from the generator at the same time as the spumy and viscous matter; it follows that, although most liquid, the sperm of the Demon, being never-

theless material, can very well mix with the material spirit of the human sperm, and bring about generation.

108. It will be retorted that, if the generation of Giants had really come from the combined sperms of Incubi and Women, Giants would still be born in our time, since there is no lack of women who have intercourse with Incubi, as is shown by the Acts of St Bernard and Peter of Alcantara, and other stories related by various authors.

109. I reply that, as has been said above, Nr 81, from Guaccius, some of those Demons are earthly, some aqueous, some aerial, some igneous, and they all dwell in their respective element. Now, it is well known that animals are of larger size, according to the element they live in; thus with fishes, many of which are diminutive, it is true, as happens with animals that live on land; but, the element water being larger than the element earth, since the container is always larger than the contents, fishes as a species, surpass in size the animals that dwell on land, as shown by whales, tunnies, cachalots, and other cetaceous and viviparous fish which surpass by far all animals that live on land. Consequently, the Demons being animals, as has been shown, their size will be proportionate to the extent of the element they dwell in, according to their nature. And, air being more extensive than water, and fire than air, it follows that ethereal and igneous Demons will by far surpass their earthly and aqueous fellows, both in stature and might. It would be to no purpose to instance, as an objection, birds which, although inhabitants of the air, a more extensive element than water, are smaller, as a species, than fishes and quadrupeds; for, if birds do indeed travel through the air by means of their wings, they no less belong to the element earth, where they rest; otherwise, some fishes that fly, such as the sea swallow, would have to be classed among aerial animals, which is not.

110. Now, it must be observed that, after the flood, the air which surrounds our earthy and aqueous globe, became, from the damp of the waters, thicker than it had been before; an, damp being the principle of corruption, that may be the reason why men do not live as long as they did before the flood. It is also on account of that thickness of the air that ethereal and igneous Demons, more corpulent than the others, can no longer dwell in that thick atmosphere, and if they do descend into it occasionally, do so only by force, much as divers descend into the depths of the sea.

111. Before the flood, when the air was not yet so thick, Demons came upon earth and had intercourse with women, thus procreating Giants whose stature was nearly equal to that of the Demons, their fathers. But now it is not so: the Incubi Demons who approach women are aqueous and of small stature; that is why they appear in the shape of little men, and, being aqueous, they are most lecherous. Lust and damp go together: Poets have depicted Venus as born of the sea, in order to show, as explained by Mythologists, that lust takes its source in damp. When, therefore, Demons of short stature impregnate women nowadays, the children that are born are not giants, but men of ordinary size. It should, moreover, be known

that when Demons have carnal intercourse with women in their own natural body, without having recourse to any disguise or artifice, the women do not see them, or if they do, see but an almost doubtful, barely sensible shadow, as was the case with the female we spoke of, Nr 28, who, when embraced by an Incubus, scarcely felt his touch. But, when they want to be seen by their mistresses, *atque ipsis delectationem in congressu carnali afferre*, they assume a visible disguise and a palpable body. By what means this is effected, is their secret, which our short-sighted Philosophy is unable to discover. The only thing we know is that such disguise or body could not consist merely in concrete air, since this must take place through condensation, and therefore by the influence of cold; a body thus formed would feel like ice, *et ita in coitu mulieres non delectaret*, but would give them pain; and it is the reverse that takes place.

112. Being admitted the distinction between spiritual Demons, which have intercourse with witches, and Incubi, who have to do with women that are nowise witches, we have to weigh the grievousness of the crime in both cases.

113. The intercourse of witches with Demons, from its accompanying circumstances, apostasy from the Faith, worshiping of the Devil, and so many other ungodly things related above, Nrs 12 to 24, is the greatest of all sins which can be committed by man; and, considering the enormity against Religion which is presupposed by coition with the Devil, Demoniality is assuredly the most heinous of all carnal crimes. But, taking the sin of the flesh as such, exclusive of the sins against Religion, Demoniality should be reduced to a simple pollution. The reason is, and a most convincing one, that the Devil who has to do with witches is a pure spirit, has reached the goal and is damned, as has been said above; if, therefore, he copulates with witches, it is in a body assumed or made by himself, according to the common opinion of Theologians. Though set in motion, that body is not a living one; and it follows that the human being, male or female, *coiens cum tali corpore*, is guilty of the same offence as if copulating with an inanimate body or a corpse, which would be simple pollution, as we have shown elsewhere. It has, moreover, been truly observed by Cajetanus, that such intercourse can very well carry with it the disgraceful characteristics of other crimes, according to the body assumed by the Devil, and the part used: thus, if he should assume the body of a kinswoman or of a nun, such a crime would be incest or sacrilege; if coition took place in the shape of a beast, or *in vase proepostero*, it would be Bestiality or Sodomy.

114. As for intercourse with an Incubus, wherein is to be found no element, not even the least, of an offence against Religion, it is hard to discover a reason why it should be more grievous than Bestiality and Sodomy. For, as we have said above, if Bestiality is more grievous than Sodomy, it is because man degrades the dignity of his kind by mixing with a beast, of a kind much inferior to his own. But, when copulating with an Incubus, it is quite the reverse: for the Incubus, by reason of his rational and immortal spirit, is equal to man; and, by reason of his body, more noble because more subtle, he is more perfect and more dignified than man. Consequently, when having intercourse with an Incubus, man does not degrade,

but rather dignifies his nature; and, taking that into consideration, Demoniality cannot be more grievous than Bestiality.

115. It is, however, commonly held to be more grievous, and the reason I take to be this: that it is a sin against Religion to hold any communication with the Devil, either with or without compact, for instance by being habitually or familiarly connected with him, by asking his assistance, counsel or favor, or by seeking from him the revelation of things to be, the knowledge of things gone by, absent, or otherwise hidden. Thus, men and women, by mixing with Incubi, whom they do not know to be animals but believe to be devils, sin through intention, *ex conscientia erronea*, and their sin is intentionally the same, when having intercourse with Incubi, as if such intercourse took place with devils; in consequence, the grievousness of their crime is exactly the same.

# Appendix

The manuscript of *Demoniality* breaks off with the conclusion just given. In a purely philosophical and theoretical acception, the work is complete: for it was enough that the author should define, in general terms, the grievousness of the crime, without concerning himself with the proceedings which were to make out the *proof*, nor with the *penalty* to be inflicted. Both these questions, on the contrary, had, as a matter of course, a place assigned to them in the great work *De Delictis et Poenis*, which is a veritable *Code for the Inquisitor*; and Father Sinistrari of Ameno could not fail to treat them there with all the care and conscientiousness he has so amply shown in the foregoing pages.

The reader will be happy to find here that practical conclusion to *Demonialiy*.

*(Note by the Editor.)*

# PROOF OF DEMONIALITY

## SUMMARY

1. *Distinctions to be made in the proof of the crime of Demoniality.*
2. *Signs proving the intercourse of a Witch with the Devil.*
3. *The confession of the Sorcerer himself is requisite for a full eviction.*
4. *Tale of a Nun who had an intimacy with an Incubus.*
5. *If the indictment is supported by the recitals of eye-witnesses, torture may be resorted to.*

As regards the proof of that crime, a distinction must be made of the kind of Demoniality, to wit: whether it is that which is practiced by Witches or Wizards with the Devil, or that which other persons perpetrate with Incubi.

In the first case, the compact entered into with the Devil being proved, the evidence of the *Demoniality* follows as a necessary consequence; for, the purpose, both of Witches and Wizards, in the nightly revels that take place after feasting and dancing, in none other but that infamous intercourse; otherwise there can be no witness of that crime, since the Devil, visible to the Witch, escapes the sight of others. Sometimes, it is true, women have been seen in the woods, in the fields, in the groves, lying on their backs, *ad umbilicum tenus nudatoe, et juxta dispositionem actus venerei,* their legs *divaricates et adductis, clunes agitare,* as is written by Guaccius, book 1, chap. 12, v. *Sciendum est soepius,* fol. 65. In such a case there would be a very strong suspicion of such a crime, if supported by other signs; and I am inclined to believe that such action, sufficiently proved by witnesses, would justify the Judge in resorting to torture in order to ascertain the truth; especially if, shortly after that action, a sort of black smoke had been seen to issue from the woman, and she had been noticed to rise, as is also written by Guaccius; for it might be inferred that that smoke or shadow had been the Devil himself, *concumbens cum foemina.* Likewise if, as has more than once happened, according to the same author, a woman had been seen *concumbere cum homine,* who, the action over, suddenly disappeared.

Moreover, in order to prove conclusively that a person is a Wizard or a Witch, the own confession of such person is requisite: for there can be no witnesses to the fact, unless perhaps other Sorcerers giving evidence at the trial against their accomplices; from their being confederates in the crime, their statement is not conclusive and does not justify the recourse to torture, should not other indications be forthcoming, such as the seal of the Devil stamped on their body, as aforesaid, Nr 23, or the finding in their dwelling, after a search, of signs and instruments of the diabolic art: for instance, bones and, especially, a skull, hair artfully plaited, intricate knots of feathers, wings, feet or bones of bats, toads or serpents, unfamiliar seeds, wax figures, vessels filled with unknown powder, oil or ointments, etc., as are usually detected by Judges who, upon a charge being brought against Sorcerers, proceed to their apprehension and the search of their houses.

The proof of intimacy with an Incubus offers the same difficulty; for, no less than other Demons, the Incubus is, at will, invisible to all but his mistress. Yet, it has not seldom happened that Incubi have allowed themselves to be surprised in the act of carnal intercourse with women, now in one shape, now in another.

In a Monastery (I mention neither its name nor that of the town where it lies, so as not to recall to memory a past scandal), there was a Nun, who, about trifles, as is usual with women and especially with nuns, had quarreled with one of her mates who occupied a cell adjoining to hers. Quick at observing all the doings of her enemy, this neighbor noticed, several days in succession, that instead of walking with her companions in the garden after dinner she retired to her cell, where she locked herself in. Anxious to know what she could be doing there all that time, the inquisitive Nun betook herself also to her cell. Soon she heard a sound, as of two voices conversing in subdued tones, which she could easily do, since the two cells were divided but by a slight partition), then a peculiar friction, the cracking of a bed, groans and sighs, *quasi duorum concumbentium*; her curiosity was raised to the highest pitch, and she redoubled her attention in order to ascertain who was in the cell. But having, three times running, seen no other nun come out but her rival, she suspected that a man had been secretly introduced and was kept hidden there. She went and reported the thing to Abbess, who, after holding counsel with discreet persons, resolved upon hearing the sounds and observing the indications that had been denounced her, so as to avoid any precipitate or inconsiderate act. In consequence, the Abbess and her confidents repaired to the cell of the spy, and heard the voices and other noises that had been described. An inquiry was set on foot to make sure whether any of the Nuns could be shut in with the other one; and the result being in the negative, the Abbess and her attendants went to the door of the closed cell, and knocked repeatedly, but to no purpose: the Nun neither answered, nor opened. The Abbess threatened to have the door broken in, and even ordered a convert to force it with a crowbar. The Nun then opened her door: a search was made and no one found. Being asked with whom she had been talking, and the why and wherefore of the bed cracking, of the sighs, etc., she denied everything.

But, matters going on just the same as before, the rival Nun, become more attentive and more inquisitive than ever, contrived to bore a hole through the partition so as to be able to see what was going on inside the cell; and what should she see but an elegant youth lying with the Nun, and the sight of whom she took care to let the others enjoy by the same means. The charge was soon brought before the bishop: the guilty Nun endeavoured still to deny all; but, threatened with the torture she confessed having had an intimacy with an Incubus.

When, therefore, indications are forthcoming, such as those recited above, a charge might be brought after a searching inquiry; yet, without the confession of the accused, the offence should not be regarded as fully proved, even if the intercourse were testified by eye-witnesses; for it sometimes happens that, in order to undo an innocent female, the Devil feigns such intercourse by means of some delusion. In those cases, the Ecclesiastical Judge must consequently trust but his own eyes.

# About the Author

Ludovico Maria Sinistrari was born in Ameno, Italy on February 26th, 1622 and died in 1701 at the age of 79. A Roman Catholic priest, theologian and prominent exorcist of his time, Rev. Father Sinistrari wrote a number of influential books on demonology and served as an advisor to the Supreme Sacred Congregation of the Roman and Universal Inquisition. After studying in Pavia, he entered the Franciscan Order in 1647 and eventually taught philosophy and theology. He achieved notoriety with his books, which delved into the intricate details of copulation with demonic forces and every type of sexual sin. As an exorcist, he postulated that demons were corporeal and were able to reproduce with human beings. He also claimed that demons had souls that could be saved. As an exorcist, he was often exposed to demonic possession and related first hand accounts of exorcisms. A trained academic and herbalist, he often experimented with formulas of herbs in conjunction with elements and bodily humors, to counter demonic activity. Rev. Father Sinistrari was notable for his attempts to use deductive reasoning, scripture, mythology and his knowledge of the natural world, in order to cure the demonic phenomena plaguing his community.